"Donlon's *Spiritual Direction for Writers* is wise and compassionate—an essential guidebook for anyone working at the intersection of the ordinary and the sacred."

—**Jamie Quatro**, author of *Two-Step Devil* and *Fire Sermon*

"In *Spiritual Direction for Writers*, Charlotte Donlon guides writers back to the deeper 'why' beneath the work. . . . This is a book I would place directly into the hands of the writers I work with, especially those navigating doubt, isolation, and creative fatigue, as a reminder that their voice is worthy of care, attention, and meaning."

—**Emely Rumble**, author of *Bibliotherapy in the Bronx*

"An inspiring, insightful offering of both practical and spiritual guidance on our writing journeys to help us navigate and nurture the gift of writing practice as art, expression, breath. This brilliant book recommends useful methods and tools to help unleash fruitful writing with purpose and vision; it helps us channel abstract philosophy about writing into tangible routine, communication, realization."

—**Jose Hernandez Diaz**,
author of *Bad Mexican, Bad American*

"At The Porch, we believe that writing is for everyone. Within that expansive definition, we recognize that the journey of the writing life requires faith, however you define it and by whatever means you nurture it. . . . Drawing from the words and wisdom of authors such as Toni Morrison, Simone Weil, Hanif Abdurraqib, Kaveh Akbar, and many more, Donlon's work will help light any writer's way."

—**Susannah Felts**, codirector of The Porch and
author of *This Will Go Down on Your Permanent Record*

"What Charlotte Donlon has given us in these pages is not simply a book on craft but an invitation to become more fully alive. This book manages to be both deeply practical and a portal into mystery. It should be a constant presence on the desk of every writer."

—**Drew Jackson**, author of
God Speaks Through Wombs and *Touch the Earth*

"How might the insights, rhythms, and rituals of spiritual practice be helpful to complicated creatives who sometimes get stuck or lose heart when facing an empty page? Drawing on her own rich experience, Charlotte Donlon shows that writing, when embraced with our whole spiritual selves, can deepen our belonging and becoming as writers and as humans. Writers will find in Donlon a gentle and encouraging guide to craft and daily life."

—**Dorothy C. Bass**, author of *Receiving the Day: Christian Practices for Opening the Gift of Time* and *Stepmother: Redeeming a Disdained Vocation*

"In *Spiritual Direction for Writers*, Charlotte Donlon has done some inspired 'bestowing' of her own, and I feel immensely blessed to be on the receiving end of its abundant practical wisdom and pastoral depth. It's so easy to get bogged down; this book carries freedom in its wings, creative as well as spiritual—highly recommended."

—**David Zahl**, author of *Seculosity* and
The Big Relief: The Urgency of Grace for a Worn-Out World

"In these pages, you will find both a holy call to action and a divine permission slip you didn't know you needed."

—**Javacia Harris Bowser**, founder of See Jane Write and author of *Find Your Way Back: How to Write Your Way Through Anything*

Spiritual Direction for Writers

Everyday Rituals for Your Writing Life

Charlotte Donlon

Here Below Books
GRAND RAPIDS, MICHIGAN

Here Below Books is an imprint of
Wm. B. Eerdmans Publishing Co.
2006 44th Street SE, Grand Rapids, MI 49508
herebelowbooks.com

Published 2026
Printed in the United States of America

32 31 30 29 28 27 26 1 2 3 4 5 6 7

ISBN 978-0-8028-8346-9

Library of Congress Cataloging-in-Publication Data

A catalog record for this book is available from the Library of Congress.

For LW and TD

Contents

Foreword

Sometimes the hardest part of being a writer isn't navigating the business, it isn't learning all the forms and styles of writing, and it isn't even killing your darlings. The hardest part, often, is to begin. Sometimes, the page feels lonely. Sometimes, it's hard to find stillness and quiet inside yourself. And, sometimes, there is help—for me, God is always there with me to help me make it through the writing process. Sometimes, God sends friends and loved ones to help us along.

Charlotte Donlon's *Spiritual Direction for Writers* is that friend, that connection to self, and that partner on the page. This book is gentle in its encouragement, and it gives real, useful advice from Charlotte's own experiences, but also from writers like Toni Morrison, Margaret Walker, and Kaveh Akbar. This type of close look at other writers is so crucial in building a writing life, which, as Charlotte points out, is "all of life." As a beginning writer, many years ago, it was vital that I understood the humanity of all the writers I admired—that they created the work which made me feel like I belonged, just like the work I am trying to create, as an exercise of self-discovery and stillness. They, too, had to find out where to begin, where to dive in, where to pause, and where to begin again. None of us is above the process, and none of us can shortcut the process. And, the process, as we find through the journey of this book, is also a vital part of writing—the time for breath, reflection, confusion, redirection, starting and starting over is time very well spent. All parts of the process yield fruit—Toni Morrison didn't write *The Bluest Eye* in a stroke of prophetic vision—first, she went to the writing group for the food!

As a writer who values the spiritual nature of the writing practice, I particularly appreciate that this book leaves room for all definitions of spirit. There is no religious prescription, there is no requirement to see the spirit/soul/world in the same way, and that truly opens up this book to a spirit connection with so many writers. Just as she is in real life, Charlotte's book makes space; supports readers, writers, and listeners; and truly *cares* about the people who encounter its pages. It is a place to land and rest, a place to be curious, to experiment, to pray, to breathe, to feel, and to embrace the truth of your identity as a writer.

—Ashley M. Jones
Poet Laureate Emerita of Alabama

A Prefatory Note

Spiritual direction, says Father James Martin, includes "empathetic listening, paying attention, affirming, assisting in clarification, raising questions." Such qualities form the heart of a process that is less about giving instructions and more about creating a sacred space for attentive presence. "A spiritual director," Father Martin adds, "doesn't direct as much as listen and notice, and help the directee listen and notice."[1]

For fourteen years, I have received spiritual direction—first from a wonderful priest, then from a canny Benedictine nun, and now from a Jungian Presbyterian who pastored local churches for two decades before turning more fully to soul care. Shortly after becoming a spiritual director myself, I found I was most drawn to working with writers. My training taught me that giving spiritual direction would nourish not just my directees but also my own soul—and, indeed, in the eight years since I began seeing writers in spiritual direction, companioning them has nurtured both my spiritual life and my writing practice.

I am always astonished by the ways God shows up during spiritual direction, each meeting with a directee reminding me that the Spirit is within and around us. Practicing spiritual direction with writers has given me intimate glimpses and more sustained gazes into the intricacies of the creative process, and in turn these glimpses and gazes have strengthened my belief that all of life is the writing life—that we are always being formed to do the writing we will do. The words we have written and will write graze the hems of epiphany, mundanity, and everything in between.

The writers I've met with have shown me how tightly faith and creativity are intertwined, even (and especially) when the divine feels absent. They long to deepen their awareness of where the spiritual and the creative realms overlap. Part of this process involves recognizing how all aspects of their life—from morning rituals to making dinner, from prayer to parenting—are integral to their lives *as writers*. Participating in spiritual direction is an opportunity to step away from worries, roles, and responsibilities, allowing writers to attend to their spiritual life and creative expression.

While it's no substitute for one-on-one spiritual direction, in this book I invite you to cultivate the same kind of contemplative space I seek to help my directees cultivate. Though we might never meet, I hope these pages will give you a meaningful experience that long-term spiritual direction provides.

Three Blessings

First, a "real writer" is anyone who writes.

If you hesitate to call yourself a writer because you don't write every day, please cease that nonsense. (Best heard with my Alabama drawl.) When asked about their creative practices, celebrated writers describe a wide variety of approaches to the page. Some write every day; some only write on the weekends. Some pass long seasons of fallow time between books or poems. Some writers work best during focused retreats. There are as many different writing rhythms as there are writers.

And there are as many reasons to write as there are writers. Some of us write for pay, write to publish, and write to inform. Others write for less public reasons. The joys and trials of writing are similar regardless. Here's one thing that's true for all writers: Moving toward more freedom in your writing and your creative identity will always invite you into holistic liberation and a wider embrace of "your one wild and precious life." Always. But you get to define what freedom means within the context of your own experiences and aspirations.

May this book help you along your unique journey.

Second, the writing life and the spiritual life go hand in hand. Both are modes and practices of inquiry and discovery. While I write from a Christian perspective, writers from diverse faith backgrounds are welcome in my spiritual-direction offerings and in these pages. Throughout the book, to create space for various understandings of the sacred, I often use the phrase "the divine" when referring to God; I also sometimes speak of God and Jesus, which are important ways that I name the divine in my own prayer life.

May you feel at ease as you read my words and contemplate your own relationship with the divine.

Finally, all of life is the writing life. This mantra is central to my work, and it makes an appearance throughout the book. When you aren't sure if you should keep writing or if your writing matters, I invite you to whisper this sentence to yourself a few times and see where this affirmation takes your mind and soul.

May you discover how all of your life feeds your writing life.

Before We Begin

of the beginning of the beginning
who spoke the tale?
you did, you did

—Kaveh Akbar

Before you write, there is silence. Before silence, there is breath. Before breath, there is being.

The space before writing begins with both absence and presence—the blank page waiting to be filled, the thoughts not yet formed, the words hovering just beyond reach. Like dawn's presence before daylight, ideas shimmer and glow golden at the edge of consciousness before taking shape on the page. We stand at this glistening threshold, this sacred space full of possibility.

To come before something is to acknowledge both separation and connection. When we sit before a desk or at the kitchen table after dinner or with a spiral notebook on a bus, we bring our whole selves. We carry our doubts and desires alongside our questions, quandaries, hopes, and hesitations. We come as we are, standing in the presence of whatever bright spark ignites our creativity.

In spiritual direction, we learn to honor the "before" moments. A pause before speaking and a breath before beginning allow us to notice the stillness before insight arrives. These spaces aren't empty but are pregnant with potential, like the moment before pen touches paper or fingers meet keys. Invitations to further noticing are everywhere along the border between intention and action.

"Before" carves sacred corners in ordinary time. Whether we're writing in stolen moments between obligations or during carefully husbanded hours free from interruption, each beginning holds the weight of the past and the lightness of what's possible. We write with and before others who have written, with and before our readers, with and before the divine who holds all our words and worlds.

Every "before" is both an ending and a beginning where preparation meets possibility. Here, in this moment, we commit our full selves to the page, ready to receive whatever gifts await in the sacred act of writing.

Pause
with Toni Morrison

"I feel more friendly when I am writing, nicer to people, much more generous, also wiser." So said Toni Morrison in a 2009 interview while describing what she experienced when she was writing often. "I am full of a kind of tenderness toward people and all they have to hide, all they have to construct. . . . The job of being a human is so hard, and it is the only job there is left—though we keep on pretending otherwise."[1]

Consistent writing made Morrison a better, kinder person, in the whole of her life. Writers know this—when I'm avoiding the page, I'm more short-tempered with my husband and kids. When grounded in my writing practice, I'm more likely to ask about their day.

But key to Morrison's interpersonal transformation was, first, her decision to take herself more seriously as a writer. To understand herself as a writer. To commit to herself as a writer. In a 2016 speech, she described the first time she attended a monthly writing group. "I went, and they had the best food you could imagine. They really put out a spread. So, I was very enchanted with that." She soon realized she'd have to generate some new work if she wanted to return. "I brought a little essay that I had written as an undergraduate, or something, and they said, 'uh huh, uh huh.' And then it became clear that I could not get any more food if I didn't have something new."[2]

After Morrison returned home, she began to consider what she could write for the following month, and a decades-old memory returned to her—"and what it meant, not just what happened, but what it meant." The memory was about a childhood friend, and what that friend told her about eye color, prayer, and God's existence. Being present to this memory opened up Morrison's imagination and curiosity. With tenacity—and at least one instance of her young son's spit-up landing on the top page of her yellow legal pad—she wrote a story she wanted to read. She developed a narrative around and in between the other portions of her life, and she took something new to her writing group each month. A story sparked by her friend's insistence that God doesn't exist eventually became her first book, *The Bluest Eye*.

Morrison didn't begin writing more seriously because she had things to write about. Instead, she "was enchanted" by platters of what might've been typical mid-1960s party food—perhaps a homemade cheese ball, Benedictine spread with crudité, a grasshopper cocktail, Watergate cake.

She began writing because she wanted to enjoy delicious food with other writers. Perhaps you, too, have experienced a similar welcoming atmosphere that stirred your senses and made you want more of that particular brand of camaraderie. What comes to mind? A potluck dinner with high school friends you haven't seen in years? A celebration with work colleagues at an iconic burger joint?

On Toni Morrison's birthday a few years ago, I came across a video of the beloved author in conversation with Frank McCourt. The clip opens with the host relaying a question from the audience, "How do you survive, whole, in a world where we are all victims of something?" The question startles, doesn't it? Especially if you want to be a whole person who seems perpetually tipped toward the tragic. Especially if you write because it helps you survive the various forms of suffering we each face.

Morrison repeats the question carefully—perhaps stalling for time as she gathers her thoughts. Then, finally: "Sometimes you don't survive whole; you just survive in part." Watching her, I exhaled, unaware I'd been holding my breath. Did she just say wholeness isn't a prerequisite for survival?

When I started breathing again, I began to release something I'd been holding on to. Has wholeness always been an impossible goal? Who made wholeness a requirement for flourishing? Do too-high expectations or goals for life and the writing life and everything else prevent one from gaining whatever the present, imperfect circumstances are offering?

Morrison continues:

> But the grandeur of life is that attempt; it's not about that solution. It is about being as fearless as one can and behaving as beautifully as one can under completely impossible circumstances. It's that that makes it elegant.
>
> Good is just more interesting. More complex. More demanding. Evil is silly. It may be horrible,

> but at the same time, it's not a compelling idea. It's predictable. . . .
>
> But the opposite, which is survival, blossoming, endurance, those things are just more compelling intellectually, if not spiritually, and they certainly are spiritually. . . .
>
> We are already born. We are going to die. So, you have to do something interesting that you respect in between.

There's a beat of silence before the host answers for all of us: "That was wild. I like that."

Yes, it's wild. Maybe my desire for wholeness of mind—to not live with bipolar disorder or ADHD—is a distraction. Perhaps my desire for wholeness of body—my worries about getting the flu this winter, my vexed relationship with exercise—keeps me from recognizing the goodness of embodiment right now while I'm relatively healthy. And what about this constant longing for a wholeness of soul that places kindness first and holds a patience with no limits—something that's not even possible on this side of eternity? Oh, how I wish I could say with assurance that I'd never share another careless social media post or let past wounds determine future reactions. What do I do with my desire for additional time to read and write? We wonder if our clocks are broken, too, while attempts to mend our minutes and hours often fall short. It's natural to long for the ideal and to wish for things to be the way they are *supposed to be*. But what if surviving in part, while moving closer toward wholeness, is itself a kind of flourishing?

With Morrison's words echoing, a new thought began to awaken: Writing and the work of being a writer are worthy of our time and attention in this space between being born and dying. The ability to endure remains even when one's circumstances are far from ideal. *Some* flourishing—even if it's barely discernible to you or others—still qualifies as flourishing.

That day I drank several cups of tea and watched a dozen more videos of Morrison discussing all manner of writerly things: reading as a revolutionary act, sitting with secrets, and prioritizing creative work as a parent. I noticed which words she repeated and emphasized—"fear*less*," "*fas*cinating," "re*spect*."[3]

When Morrison was growing up, she worked an after-school job as a housekeeper for a wealthy woman whose home contained luxuries uncommon in Morrison's neighborhood—"a plastic-covered sofa and chairs, wall-to-wall blue-and-white carpeting," and other marks of privilege. One day, feeling frustrated by her employer's increasing demands, she complained to her father in their kitchen.

Rather than offering escape, her father gave perspective that would shape her entire approach to work and identity. He put his coffee cup down on the table and said, "Listen. You don't live there. You live here. With your people." Then he offered these simple instructions: "Go to work. Get your money. And come on home." This conversation taught Morrison lasting lessons about doing good work for yourself and making the job rather than letting it make you, while being intentional about the choices that form your real life.

In reflecting on this pivotal moment, Morrison wrote, "I have worked for all sorts of people since then, geniuses and morons, quick-witted and dull, bighearted and narrow . . . but since that conversation with my father I have never considered the level of labor to be the measure of myself, and I have never placed the security of a job above the value of home."[4]

Morrison is more than just a celebrated author and editor—I think she can serve as an unofficial spiritual guide for writers seeking to understand the relationship between creativity and inner life. Her work demonstrates how writing opens the soul and draws from our deepest wells, even if no one would call our writing devotional or even particularly pious. As we navigate the breadth and depth of creative life, spiritual direction offers the kind of guidance Morrison's father provided: helping us remember who we are, where we live, and what matters most.

I invite you to pause here to reflect on Morrison's wisdom about identity, work, and home. What parts of your writing life feel like "living there" versus "living here"? Where do you find your true creative home?

Take a moment to sit with her words about survival and wholeness. Perhaps write in your journal about what it means to you that "sometimes you don't survive whole; you just survive in part." How might accepting this truth free you to write from wherever you are right now?

Finally, reflect on Morrison's observation that writing made her "more friendly . . . nicer to people, much more generous, also wiser." How does your writing practice shape who you are beyond the page? What aspects of your creative work help you navigate "the job of being human"?

These questions aren't meant to be answered quickly but are rather to be carried with you as companions on your writing journey. Like the sage words from Morrison's father, they can help you remember what matters most as you move between your roles and responsibilities and recognize how all of life is the writing life.

Belong, Become, Behold, Bestow

Several months ago, I polled people via social media about why they write. More than a hundred responses rolled in over the course of a few days, including: "I write to find my secret self—to upset others' unwelcome false projections of me. I write to touch God—even just, at best, the shadow of the hem. I write to awaken many dormant worlds within."

"To clarify and record my own thinking and contribute to the ongoing conversation with others."

"Because [writing] calls to me."

One of the reasons we write is to belong. "To find my secret self" is one way to belong to the self. "Contribute to the ongoing conversation with others" expresses a desire to belong to others and the larger world. "Writing calls to me" describes belonging to the divine.

When you write—and it doesn't matter whether it's a novel or a poem, a diary entry or a Substack note—you gain greater self-awareness and self-knowledge. You discover more commonalities between yourself and others. You discern a broader invitation into new and different realms of the world. You realize the divine is more present and approachable. Gaining a greater sense of belonging remains my first reason to write and continues to pique my curiosity when discussing this vocation and calling with others.

That said, belonging will never be the only reason to write. One reason Toni Morrison wrote was because she learned at a very early age about the power of words.[1] Rebecca Solnit writes because she refuses to be silenced by others.[2] Another reason I write is because I enjoy it. It's fun.

Over the course of one week, not that long ago, I met with six different writers. They shared different reasons for meeting with me for one-on-one spiritual direction. But despite their differences, all six of them—and every writer I've ever had a spiritual direction session with—said that writing helps them feel less alone. When they write, they are more fully themselves. Awareness of the intersection of their spirituality and creativity grows, as well as their ability to notice how those connections affect their relationships, desires, hopes, and fears. When they write, barriers to the divine dissolve, even if they aren't entirely sure what they believe. Even if their doubts outnumber their convictions.

As your belongings shift and settle and shift again in different seasons of life, you may notice additional ways writing helps you feel less alone. You might perceive how your writing practice forms you to become someone new, someone you weren't last week, last month, last year. You are always becoming who you will be when you write the next letter, essay, poem, or story. While this process of becoming is forming who you are when you write, the act of writing, in turn, affects who you are, who you will become, and how you are being formed. When our belongings deepen and our becomings broaden, our beholdings expand. Seeing the world with more clarity brings a more frequent bestowing of good things on oneself and others through writing.

Imagine writing to belong, become, behold, and bestow as four points along an immense bright spiral of light with rays extending in all directions along the curving trajectories, each resplendent and brilliant. When you write what you're called to write, you bestow good things on others. When someone reads what you've written and feels less alone, you've helped them experience an expanded sense of belonging and offered something that has affected who *they* are becoming.

Even if no one reads your writing, you still offer good things to the world, because through writing, you inhabit a fuller, brighter version of yourself—one shaped and formed by the practice. Through this transformation, you grow in understanding what it means to belong. You continue becoming more of who you're meant to be, experiencing further growth as you behold so much goodness. From this sense of belonging, becoming, and beholding, generosity shines outward—you bestow gifts on yourself and others, even in ways too mysterious to see, touch, or hear.

Each point along the golden spiral of light serves as an invitation into this continuous cycle. You can enter any time through any posture of belonging, becoming, beholding, or bestowing, then dart and pulse along the spiral—upward or downward, inward or outward—as you find your way toward whatever comes next.

Whether you're writing journal entries or novels, poetry or prayers, each act of writing pulls you into this luminous cycle of belonging, becoming, beholding, and bestowing that continuously reinforces your connections to yourself, others, the divine, and your creative practice.

Begin

Another thought startles from me, a small, watery-muscled, downy-haired idea: I want to walk through a world of my own making.

—Jesmyn Ward

To begin is to trust that something waits to emerge. Like seeds sprouting in darkness, beginning contains both uncertainty and promise. We begin with each new page, every fresh paragraph, another blank screen waiting for words.

Writers know many beginnings. The beginning of morning pages[1] *while birds chirp and tea steeps. The beginning of a lyric essay when an image won't let you go. The beginning of a poem that arrives unexpectedly during a grief walk. Each start carries forward what came before while opening to what's possible.*

In spiritual direction, we learn that beginning isn't about perfection but presence. We begin where we are, as we are. Sometimes that means writing through tears, doubt, or confusion. Other times it involves showing up to the page when words feel distant. Always, we trust the process of emergence.

Beginning requires courage alongside surrender. Courage to face the blank page, to write the first word, to start again after an extended time away from the desk. Surrender to the mystery of creativity, the ways writing shapes both the work and the writer, and the divine spark that ignites imagination.

To start, to attempt, to undertake: "begin" suggests movement, initiative, the first step toward a destination.

But beginning isn't just about starting something new. It's about entering the cycle of creativity that spirals ever deeper, each beginning building on what came before.

When we gather in writing groups or swap pages with a friend, we begin together. When we sit alone at our desks at dawn, we begin in solitude. But all beginnings share this: They are acts of faith in the creative process, in our own capacity to grow, in the possibility that what emerges will carry meaning beyond ourselves.

To begin is to say yes to what calls us to the page, trusting that each new start carries us closer to who we're becoming as writers and human beings.

Begin Where You Are

One way to begin anything is to start where you are.

"In the midway of this our mortal life" is the first line of Dante's *Inferno*, a book that begins *in medias res*, or "in the midst of things." The reader is plopped down into the middle of the action without context for the character's formative history, physical setting, or where they are in the narrative arc. In the early pages of this epic, Dante, himself the poem's narrator, is lost in a forest at night and trying to find his way.[1]

Readers enter a different tangle of dark woods in the first paragraph of Jesmyn Ward's novel *Let Us Descend*. The narrator describes a childhood memory of her mother waking her in the middle of the night and taking her "deep, deep into the murmuring trees, black with the sun's leaving." The two trek far from a house of harm, away from the man whose skin is as white as the mother's is dark. They flee this man who believes he owns them.[2]

Both stories begin in the depth of night in a wooded thicket. Both begin in the middle of the action. Dante's narrator is disoriented and navigating a gloomy and dangerous space. Ward's narrator knows exactly where she is and that her mother is ushering her to a place of safety.

One way to begin *writing* is to start where you are. Even if where you are is a dark forest.

It's easy to believe that, to move forward with our work, we need a grand beginning to a perfect writing session. A brilliant idea with plenty of energy. Four hours uninterrupted. A deliciously quiet house. A cheering section full of social media followers telling us how talented we are and reminding us that our art matters. But if we wait for ideal circumstances to write, we'll spend more time waiting than writing.

Writers can establish a nourishing creative practice by beginning where they are rather than waiting for perfect conditions or following a list of rigid rules about what it means to be a "real writer." Where are you right now? What's going on in and around you? Are the stars aligned just so? If they are, please stop reading immediately and go write!

If the stars remain askew, can you begin writing where you are anyway, even if it's the middle of the woods in the middle of the night? Can you trust that regardless of the current state of your writing life, everything you have experienced, learned, and noticed up to this point has brought you to where you need to be to write whatever you can write right now? Can you begin in the middle of this present moment? What if this moment matters, too? What would happen if you chose to let this middle be a worthy beginning?

A novel or poem can open *in medias res*, and so can a writing session.

I invite you to let go of any anxieties that are holding you back and be open to whatever your curiosity, knowledge, and experiences have ushered you toward. Be exactly who you are and where you are in this middle. Let this middle begin in danger or safety. Let it begin with knowing or not knowing. Let it begin whether you face obstacles or a clear path to safety.

Whatever you don't have yet can wait. The perfect laptop, notebook, pen, feedback, validation. The preferred hour, day, month, year, weather, season. All of it can wait. You can begin in the middle of whatever is already unfolding.

Take your notebook or pen outside, or sit by a window. Take notes for ten minutes on what you see around you and what those observations can help you know. Tune in to your senses. Describe the temperature, weather, season. Be more specific about this portion of this season. Is it midwinter? Early spring? Late summer? What do you remember of this particular season from years past? Take a deep inhale. What does your sense of smell tell you? Capture a few memories that emerge. Shift your gaze to another direction. Over there. Jot down a few items from this line of sight. Look up at the sky. Look down at the ground. Move closer. What else do you notice?

Begin with a New Perspective

During the difficult pandemic months of the summer and autumn of 2020, the realization that all of life is the writing life transformed my understanding of creativity and spirituality. My father died in August 2020 from COVID-19, and my first book came out in November 2020. So, those intense months were difficult in a way I'd never experienced before. The plan that I'd concocted for the book's publication was moot once the pandemic hit. And my grief was consuming. Most hours of most days following my father's death included little more than weeping and sleeping. I wondered if I would ever write again.

To retain some hope for the future of my writing practice, I needed a new narrative about the creative process that was true all the time—not just during the months when writing was going well. I had to believe that all the grief and rest and weeks of not writing mattered to the creative process, and I began to see that all of life is the writing life. While we aren't actively writing, we are being formed to be the people we will be when the time to write again presents itself. While we aren't actively writing, we are experiencing things that will influence our future work.

This notion has accompanied me out of the dramatic grief following my father's death and into and through more mundane fallow periods. If you aren't writing as much as you want to for whatever reason—well, that could be because you're resisting something, or because you simply don't feel like writing, or because the demands of earning a living are consuming, or because caregiving leaves you little time and space. In all those circumstances, the truth that all of life is the writing life prevails. The resistance you're battling is shaping you. Whatever's happening that reduces your desire to write is teaching you. This resistance or lack of energy for your work is a necessary component of the writing that you will do when it's time to return to the page.

When we embrace the idea that who we are right now is forming who we will be and the art we will make in the future, we inhabit the writing life in healthier ways that nourish our full selves. Regardless of whether we write on a particular day, everything counts. The creative work we are doing or not doing. The angst, rejection, failure, dread, joy, delight, wonder, fear. Every conversation, argument, postcard, prayer, meal, errand, nap, dream, nightmare. Every moment of every day and every night is forming who we will be when we write again.

The idea that all of life is the writing life allows me to continue in my writing and work today. It can help you continue in your writing and work, too. When you believe all of life is the writing life, you will find more freedom in that space where your creative practice intersects with your spirituality and beyond. You will feel less anxious. You will quit worrying so much about why you did whatever you did when you could've been writing instead.

I suspect the pattern of this insight holds true for lives beyond writing. All of life is the artist's life. All of life is the basketball life. The visual artist is becoming who she will be when it's time to piece together a new collage after she's able to sleep more than a few hours at a time following the birth of her child. The athlete is being transformed into a new version of himself that will eventually show up on the court while healing from an injury that has him benched longer than he'd like. Everything matters while we are waiting to make our art, do our work, compete for our team. As we make our way through the interruptions and disruptions, nothing is wasted.

Consider Margaret Walker's account of writing her novel *Jubilee*, which she started at the age of nineteen while an undergraduate student at Northwestern and finished thirty years later. In an interview about her writing process, Walker was asked what it was like to live with *Jubilee* for three decades. She responded, "You just become part of it, and it becomes part of you. Working, raising a family, all of that becomes part of it. Even though I was preoccupied with everyday things, I used to think about what I wanted to do with *Jubilee*." She said one of the most difficult aspects of the gap between beginning and finishing the book was the feeling that, because of various illnesses, she might not get to complete the work. "And, even if I had the time to work at it," she added, "I wasn't sure I would be able to do it the way I wanted." Walker described the time living with the book as "agonizing," but it was worth the wait: as Walker put it, "*Jubilee* is the product of a mature person. When I started out with the book, I didn't know half of what I now know about life. . . . There's a difference between writing about something and living through it. I did both."[1]

Once launched, the creative process can't be stopped any more than waves coming ashore. That movement and energy are unending, even when it doesn't feel like it. You're always inhabiting your writing practice, even if you haven't done the writing you wanted to do for the past six days, six weeks, or six months.

Several types of ocean waves exist, but the waves we see at the beach are usually created by the wind. If the wind ceases, or changes intensity or direction, the waves affected won't grow larger, but they will continue traveling. They keep traveling until they run into something like a sandy shore. That's why we always see waves at the beach, even when it's not windy. We can't stop the water from coming ashore, and we can't end our creativity.

In his book *Inspired*, Matt Richtel considers the creative process: "Ideas come to us through our default networks. They stream from the subconscious, in times of quiet, moments of inspiration, experiences of raw emotion, states of authenticity. They appear to us, often not so much willed but allowed and permitted." He describes studies that explain how ideas travel through neural pathways in the brain during times of creativity and how those ideas can begin with something as simple as seeing.[2] Yes. By opening your eyes and looking at what's around you. If you're a writer or an artist and you think your creativity is blocked or that you have somehow removed yourself from the creative process, think again. *You're still participating in the creative process*—unless you've figured out how to banish every idea and interaction with the world and keep your eyes closed tight forever and ever.

Since the creative process is continuous, it makes sense to nourish your writerly self in ways that require no writing. Maybe you need to rest for four hours or an entire Saturday. Or you want to take your lunch hour to peruse the beautiful textiles and threads in that sewing shop you've never been to because you don't sew. Maybe ice cream at that fancy dessert place beside the sewing shop sounds nice because you do eat ice cream. Or, after the kids are tucked in, you decide to grab a stack of favorite books from your shelves and climb in bed to read with a fresh pot of lemon chamomile tea on your nightstand until you can't keep your eyes open any longer.

I'm not saying you don't need to write. Writers write. You need to sit down with your laptop or notebook or journal and do your work. But everything else counts too, so you might as well honor all the things of life as genuine components of the writing life. I find that this honoring of ice cream and lemon tea helps me feel more relaxed about my writing; and if you feel more relaxed, you might just end up writing more and even *enjoy* it more. You may be more able to notice the divine in your creative work and beyond while discerning how writing helps you belong to yourself, others, and the world.

Begin with Fifteen Minutes

It's April 6, 2012, and my therapist, Julie, is giving me the look that means she's about to ask me to do something difficult. I'm worried about that look in her eyes because most things are already too hard in my current condition. The last thing I want is another task that feels impossible.

I've been meeting with Julie weekly for eight months—since I began recovering from my second manic episode and subsequent depression. During one of our early sessions, she told me getting well was my part-time job. I've been putting in the hours and have made a lot of progress, but mild-to-moderate depression shadows me every day.

I shift my focus to Julie's lips. We wear the same berry-colored gloss from Estee Lauder. I press my own lips together while she speaks: "If you're a writer and you aren't writing, you aren't going to get better."

I relax my tight jaw.

"After you get home today, write for fifteen minutes. Do it before the kids get home from school. Then write for at least fifteen minutes every day. If you don't know what to write, repeat 'I don't know what to write' again and again until more words come."

"I can do that. Thanks for not asking me to do something harder."

"Write every day. It might be harder than you think."

Fleetwood Mac's *Rumours* plays on Pandora on my way home from Julie's office. Traffic is light so I pull into the driveway during the final notes of the third song. This album has been a close companion ever since I was manic the previous summer. After "Second Hand News" and "Dreams," I skip a few tracks and listen to "The Chain." As soon as I walk through the back door, I go directly to my bedroom and climb into the unmade bed with my small notebook computer. Using a new Word document, I add April 6, 2012, to the top and start typing. My fingers keep moving for fifteen minutes. It's terrible. But I followed Julie's directions. I began in the middle of my path to becoming more of my full self, and that's a win. Any win is satisfying at this point in life.

I'd known I was a writer since I fell in love with reading books aloud to my daughter and sending group emails to my friends and family during the earliest years of motherhood. By the time my daughter could talk, she was telling stories and speaking poems. Once she could write, she slipped her stories and poems under the crack of my closed bedroom door. Witnessing her natural inclination to write inspired me to write even more. I started a blog, like so many people did back then. I didn't think of it as a mommy blog because I didn't write much about mothering. But I'm a writer because my daughter was a writer first. She showed me the way.

The bullet-pointed notes and lists from those early days of writing for fifteen minutes turned into essays that were first only for me; in time, those secrets became public pieces published by various websites, magazines, and journals. A few years later, I included some of them in my applications to master of fine arts programs. After I finished graduate school, I submitted a book proposal to various editors, then another, and another which was accepted for publication. Then I wrote my first book.

I kept writing most days for at least fifteen minutes. I became a better writer and stayed well mentally (mostly) while avoiding additional mania and significant depression for several years. Writing is no miracle cure for mental illness; I was then and continue to be in therapy and on meds to manage my mental health. But writing—and the access it gives me to a practice of belonging and becoming—has been a key component in my own personal project of being my fullest self. And I'm not alone. Others testify to the transformative power of a creative practice.

In 2021 Birmingham poet laureate Salaam Green led a session entitled "Writing to Heal" at the Magic City Poetry Festival. "What we're doing here—writing based on writing prompts, writing to heal, and poetry to heal," said Green, "is based on the process that happens as someone is writing the poem and reflecting on the emotions that came up while writing." As an artist-in-residence at Birmingham's large university hospital, Green has worked alongside doctors and nurses to care for very sick patients. She has seen how reading and writing poems supports people and opens new passageways as they navigate grief and other confusing feelings that can come with illness. As she leads others through her writing-to-heal process, she's a doula for the emotions, guiding sadness, longing, fear, gratitude, and anything else toward expression. Writing poetry—even bad poems—"calls our names," says Green. Writing helps us know more of who we are called to be and what we are called to do.[1]

Writers don't have to write one thousand words a day, or for three hours every day. We needn't follow any arbitrary rules to prove we are "real writers." Yet, if we go too long without writing, things can turn sideways. Ignoring our writing practice can be a way of ignoring ourselves, and writers can lose the essence of our full selves when we don't write.

When I don't write enough, I usually end up yelling at Tim and the kids for dumb reasons. Wonder and enchantment seem out of reach. Faith loses to doubt too often. Loneliness swells. This sort of funk may continue for a few blurry days before I realize what's happening and that a fifteen-minute writing session might straighten things out with a much-needed shift in perspective.

Today I know that Julie not only helped me embrace my role as a writer and establish a regular writing practice. She also helped me have a greater sense of belonging to myself, and she helped me learn how to honor writing's place in my overall flourishing. By following Julie's instructions, I was able to grasp a solid writerly identity and maintain it throughout various seasons and circumstances. When we cherish our identity as writers, every return to the page—even a quarter-hour return—becomes a new beginning.

Begin with Rest

During one of our last spiritual direction sessions, Samantha asked me how I give to myself what I give the writers I work with. Her question caught me off guard since I'm the one who is supposed to do the asking. But neither was I surprised that she chose to use a portion of *her* spiritual direction session to ask about *me* and *my* daily rhythms with a tone of genuine care and concern. She has a tender heart, a perceptive soul, and a curious mind.

After a brief pause to consider her question, I began speaking and rambled my way into the answer: "I rest first. Always. Giving myself what I know I need is the priority. And I know I need sufficient rest."

I could see her head nodding in agreement on the computer screen. Her eyes showed glimmers of approval. Maybe she rests first too.

Having plenty of rest nourishes me and helps me be more of the person *I* want to be. Rest nourishes you, too. So, I encourage you to consider this question: How are you giving yourself rest? Also: How do you give yourself what you give others?

The ability to rest well will evolve and develop through trial and error. As someone who lives with bipolar disorder and ADHD, I simply can't move through my days and weeks at the speed of many people around me. Well, maybe I could. But I don't want to. Not anymore.

Sidestepping the capitalistic pressures and hustle economies that value people based on what they produce keeps me healthier as a writer, a mother, a friend.

Most of us have been simmering in the you-are-what-you-do stockpot our whole lives, so it's easy to fall back into a mind-set of productivity and performance. Every now and then I'll pause when I'm in the middle of working on something on a Sunday afternoon that's deflating my energy and joy like a punctured tire losing air. I'll ask myself, "Why am I working on this tedious thing right now while I'm tired and hangry? Who's making me do this?" And I'll realize no one is making me do anything. I'll stop, go to the kitchen, and make a peanut butter sandwich. Then I'll crash into our large comfy sofa, put on a sleep mask, and take a nap. Life's too short to act as if things matter more than they really do.

Of course, from time to time we rally to the aid of a child or friend or neighbor when we are exhausted. Life still happens when we were up all night for whatever reason. We rarely have a say in how and when exigencies present themselves. But after the emergency passes, resetting and returning to a rhythm that includes rest is, for me, crucial to meeting the page.

Tricia Hersey, author of *Rest Is Resistance*, serves as an excellent guide for anyone exploring their relationship with rest. This is what happened when, as a young child, Hersey saw her grandmother "resting her eyes": "Whenever I would inquire if she was sleeping, her response was always the same: 'Every shut eye ain't sleep. I am resting my eyes and listening for what God wants to tell me.' While all the world around her was attempting to crush her Spirit, she rested and resisted the beast of grind culture."

Hersey's grandmother taught Hersey's mother to rest, and she taught Hersey how to rest. And now Hersey helps thousands, maybe millions, of people know the value of rest and "embrace rest as a way to make us all more human."[1]

When I was growing up, my mom sometimes claimed she needed to rest her eyes before promptly falling into a deep sleep within minutes of her head hitting a throw pillow on the pastel flame-stitched sofa in the den. Her use of the term "resting my eyes" was more of a way to not admit that she was completely exhausted and needed legitimate sleep, a real nap. She obviously needed to rest more than just her eyes. Her long, deep naps restored her mind and body and all the spaces in between. Then she would rise and dive right back into a pace of life and work that makes me tired just thinking about it.

Begin with Your Breath

Take a moment right now and breathe in slowly for six seconds. Now exhale at the same speed. Take another slow breath. Then settle back into your normal breathing rhythm. Follow your breath along its path. Where does it come from? Where does it go?

By the time I read James Nestor's *Breath: The New Science of a Lost Art* in the fall of 2020, I—and most people—had been giving more thought than usual to breath and breathing due to COVID-19. The pandemic invited many of us into a new relationship with our lungs, breath, inhales, and exhales. Six years later, I continue to have a growing awareness of my breathing patterns. It's easier to recognize when I'm holding my breath. I'm a pro at taking a beat to make myself let go of my jaw, neck, and shoulder muscles that store stress and serve as a sort of switch that turns off my ability to breathe well. I'm better at beginning to breathe again.

I first used breathing as a calming tool when my kids were little. I taught my son how to take ten deep breaths to regulate his emotions when his frustration overwhelmed him and his feelings were bigger than his words. Sitting next to him and bending down to his tear-streaked face, I'd put my arm around his torso and count each breath while he followed my prompts and calmed himself. Now, I'm pretty sure all those times we stopped to breathe together were also for me. I needed to take ten deep breaths as much as, if not more than, he did. Pausing to breathe was certainly more effective than losing my temper and letting my own emotions get out of control while he fell apart. I wonder if our vocabulary ever catches up with our emotions.

My favorite part of Nestor's *Breath* is a short section on how all religions from the beginning of time have prayers with the same breathing structure. Nestor writes:

> In 2001, researchers at the University of Pavia in Italy gathered two dozen subjects, covered them with sensors to measure blood flow, heart rate, and nervous system feedback, then had them recite a Buddhist mantra as well as the original Latin version of the rosary, the Catholic prayer cycle of the Ave Maria, which is repeated half by a priest and half by the congregation. They were stunned to find the average number of breaths for each cycle was "almost exactly" identical, just a bit quicker than the pace of the Hindu, Taoist, and Native American prayers: 5.5 breaths a minute.[1]

I wanted to know if this was true for me, so I timed myself a few times while repeating the most common form of the Jesus prayer, "Lord Jesus Christ, Son of God, have mercy on me, a sinner," and watched it clock in at around six seconds. I was sold. I began including a breathing exercise with six deep breaths using a six-count inhale and a six-count exhale in my own prayer and writing practices, and during spiritual direction sessions. And I began to breathe in a sixfold pattern throughout my typical days, while driving, during my walks, and when I want to pray but don't have easy access to any words. Like generations of Christians and people from other faith traditions, I've learned to simply let my breath be a prayer. A few months ago, I found myself taking deep breaths with a six-count inhale and a six-count exhale while sitting with my mom in the hospital before a minor surgery. And a few weeks ago, I turned to the same pattern while my daughter was away hiking and off the grid for four days. Breathing was better than falling into a negative spiral of worry. Yesterday the familiar rhythm of inhales and exhales returned while walking the prayer labyrinth at the church my husband and I attend. It seems I instinctively fall into this breathing pattern several times each day.

Do you want to try it? Take six deep breaths with a six-count inhale and a six-count exhale. Give your attention to your body. What changes with each new breath? What do you feel? What hurts more? What relaxes? Where do you feel energy? Where do you feel heaviness? Where do you feel lighter? What do you want to remember about your responses to these questions? Write that down.

Begin with Prayer

"Prayer consists of attention," Simone Weil writes in her essay "Reflections on the Right Use of School Studies with a View to the Love of God." "It is the orientation of all the attention of which the soul is capable toward God. The quality of the attention counts for much in the quality of prayer."[1] A prayer, then, can be any moment of mindfulness, reverence, concentration. Many people probably picture the act of prayer as a person talking to God. And because we might often think of prayer as a last resort in the midst of difficult circumstances, we likely hold in our minds the image of a supplicant like George Bailey from *It's a Wonderful Life*—alone, desperate, seeking divine intervention. In the film's climactic prayer scene, Bailey, on the brink of bankruptcy and possible imprisonment, sits in a bar by himself, tears in his eyes. He clasps his hands together to beseech a God he's not even sure is listening: "Dear Father in heaven," he says despairingly, "I'm not a praying man but if you're up there and you can hear me, show me the way. I'm at the end of my rope. Show me the way, God."[2]

"Begin with Prayer" was originally published as "Prayer Consists of Attention: On Reading as a Spiritual Practice." This essay first appeared on TheMillions.com on May 9, 2022.

I've uttered hundreds of prayers like George Bailey's, and I've prayed countless times in this most traditional sense, as "a person talking to God." But to describe the multiplicity of my own prayers now, I borrow from the language of clouds: my stratus prayers are flat and smooth, originating from the mundane things of life; my cumulus prayers billow with a fullness of faith, or doubt, or a mixture of both; my cirrus clouds are soaring and wispy with room for mystery; my alto prayers are steady and observant; and my nimbus prayers hold my tears, my grief. But the same current of profound attention animates all these prayers—I listen, watch, and wait while paying careful attention to the divine and whatever shape it takes in my life and the world around me.

If prayer is attention, perhaps the inverse is true. Can attention to an everyday activity, like reading or writing, also be prayer? That question first entered my mind as I read the last chapter of the 2021 novel *Hell of a Book*, in which Jason Mott writes about anger in a way that reads like a psalm of lament. Reflecting on the pain, loss, and oppression intrinsic to Black life in the United States, the book's protagonist, a writer who is struggling to tell the story of his life, muses: "You'll be angry and not know why. And the anger won't ever go away, not really. It'll hang in the back of your mind. It'll hang in the back of your world, haunting you, guiding all of your decisions. And when you get tired of being angry, it still won't go away. It'll just change into something even worse. You'll take that anger and turn it on yourself and it'll call itself depression. And, just like anger, it'll take over your life.

It'll live with you every day."[3] This passage evoked for me the same raw anguish of Psalm 88—

> O Lord, why do you cast me off?
> Why do you hide your face from me?
> (v. 14 NRSV)

Suddenly I could not see much difference between opening my Bible to pray Psalm 88 and reading *Hell of a Book*, or any work of literature that, like this novel, honestly approaches the realities of suffering. I realized that all words have the potential to become prayers.

Over the past few years, practicing spiritual direction with writers has given me many opportunities to think about how writing can also be prayer. During a spiritual direction session, my directees and I set apart fifty minutes to be curious about the divine. When I listen to others tell me about their writing lives and creative processes, I often hear them talk about how they notice God, how they give their attention to God, and how God feels present or absent in their work. One writer tells me how a word or phrase will come to her mind from outside herself, a gift from God, while she's writing an essay. Another shares how his writing practice flourished after he left his fundamentalist church, a decision that liberated his creative sensibilities as well as his mind and spirit.

While recently reading Victoria Chang's book *Dear Memory: Letters on Writing, Silence, and Grief*, I found myself assuming the same prayerful posture of listening and watching as I do when I'm with directees. I'm not praying *for* Chang, but I am giving her what Weil would call my "unmixed attention." In a chapter addressed to one of her writing teachers, Chang reinforces the connections I feel between reading, writing, God, and prayer. "I now think words are light," she writes. "How they illuminate the small beak of a lark isn't up to the writer. It's up to the lark and the light. A writer is just a guest, the birder."[4]

Reading these words, I consider how language and literature have illuminated my life, both supplementing and complementing my spiritual practice. And how the lark and the light could represent divine mystery, and how my bearing witness to the sliver of humanity lit up by literature helps me understand that mystery a little bit more. How, like a birder, the writer or the reader can seek out answers, but also must be patient in waiting for what they seek.

Later in her essay, Weil names the centrality of waiting. (Indeed, the essay was eventually collected in a volume titled *Attente de Dieu*—then later in English, *Waiting for God*.) "Above all our thought should be empty, waiting, not seeking anything, but ready to receive in its naked truth the object that is to penetrate it," she writes. "We do not obtain the most precious gifts by going in search of them but by waiting for them."[5] Now, when I read or write, I feel as though I too am waiting for God, for a flash of insight, or for that wholeness of soul that makes me feel more connected to myself, others, the divine, and the world. I'm no longer surprised when I look up from my book or my computer and see that I'm surrounded by a swirl of clouds.

If you pray or are curious about prayer, try reading a favorite poem, short story, or essay and consider how it might also be a prayer. Then sit in silence for five minutes.

Don't worry about what's happening in your mind or soul. Just sit in silence for five minutes and see what happens next.

Another way to pray is to linger in the space between sleeping and waking. When you first begin to stir from slumber, ask if there's anything for you to receive for your creative work, or for your sense of belonging to yourself and the divine. See what sort of magic might be waiting for you in that gap between being asleep and opening your eyes. Stay put. Be still. Don't reach for your phone or a pen and paper. Save those things for later. Take advantage of this space that your body, mind, and soul only inhabit after several hours of sleep.

Begin with Honoring the Fullness of Life

Magical things can happen when your eyes are closed and your brain is half alert, so it's nice to linger there when you can afford to do so. In that place between sleeping and waking, one morning last summer, I was turning over a few thoughts about what's at the core of my approach to spiritual direction for writers and realized I'm most interested in paying attention to how writers inhabit time and space when they *aren't* doing the writing they want to do—and in helping them find their way back to a sustainable writing practice.

All of us know the logistics of the writing life. You sit down and you write. But if it were that simple, we would all be sitting down and writing more often, probably, or we would be enjoying it more, or we wouldn't be so difficult to live with when we aren't doing it.

How can you move closer to writing an essay, poem, story, screenplay, or whatever is knocking on the door of your imagination? And what do you do with your heart, mind, and soul when you ignore the plea from your imagination, when you skip the writing you want to do, or when you decide with gusto to do something else, or when you finally sit down to write but you're interrupted again?

When the writing needs something else before you

can begin, or if it's not going the way you thought it would go, that's good information to pay attention to. Perhaps it's evidence that something else is off. Are you tired? Depleted? Sad? Do you need to grieve? Do you need to celebrate? Do you need to remember? Do you need to apologize to your kids or your colleague? Do you need to acknowledge the reality of this present moment?

This one. Right now.

Sometimes it's easier for us writers to stay in our heads than feel feelings, move our bodies, say things out loud, or discern which shift we need to make in response to the current reality.

This one. Right now.

Maybe it's time to quit worrying about the writing you aren't doing and get up and sort through that box of your mother's scarves you inherited last spring. The ones still wrapped in tissue paper, still holding traces of her perfume. The box sits in your guest room corner, taking up emotional and spiritual space. It would be better to go on and throw off your weighted blanket and get up and just go through the scarves now because the burden of postponed grief might be heavier than your creative resistance.

Becoming a better writer is a great goal. So is writing without losing your body, mind, and soul. Let's give more thought to what it means to establish practices that honor the full self. You don't need to have everything figured out before you move forward. You can write today as you are right now. You can write with your contradictions, complexities, and imperfections. Right now. Or, after you handle those scarves.

Begin with Nourishing Rhythms

Giving time to my five favorite nourishing rhythms most days, not every day, keeps me in my preferred sweet spot for all areas of life. And my flexible work schedule means that I can also adjust the frequency and duration of these central rhythms. On an ideal day, I write for two hours, read for an hour, walk for forty-five minutes, have an encounter with some form of art for at least fifteen minutes, and do a contemplative prayer practice for thirty minutes. But most days aren't ideal, so I might do each of the five rhythms for only five or ten minutes, and I'll know good things will still happen because these are the five things I do that help me feel like more of my full-writer self, my full self.

I discuss establishing nourishing rhythms with most writers to help them move closer to the writing life (or, indeed, the whole life) they want. It's always delightful to learn what nourishes each person and follow along as they experiment with various rhythms before settling on their main three or four. Some people include gardening, playing the guitar, singing, or baking. Others like to start with some of the basic rhythms that work for me—reading, writing, and walking.

You can begin by assessing what you already do on a regular basis. What do you do most days or most weeks because you enjoy life more when these activities are on your calendar? Can you develop more intentionality with the practices and rhythms that already enable you to inhabit your creativity and faith in healthy ways? Take notes or journal for ten minutes about possibilities and plans to incorporate more nourishing rhythms throughout your days and weeks. What do you want to do more of? What do you want to do less of?

One poet and essayist with two young children and a full-time job told me the most consistent thing she does to nourish herself is attend her favorite Pilates class on Saturday mornings. "The class feels like church to me."

I told her that sounded like a great rhythm for her list and asked if she wanted to stack another rhythm on top of the Pilates that was already established. "What can you add to that existing weekly rhythm that will help you have more time to do the writing you want to do? Can you leave home thirty minutes earlier with a travel mug of coffee, and then sit in your car in the Pilates studio parking lot and take notes for fifteen or twenty minutes before your class starts?"

Within a few weeks this new rhythm was going so well she added another round of coffee, notes, and Pilates on Wednesday evenings.

It can be easy to think the depleting habits you've fallen into aren't harmful. But if you can't remember the last time you sat down to write, or if you can remember and it's been way too long, it might be helpful to put yourself in the way of good things that will give you more opportunities to have the writing life you want.

May we all receive the nourishment we need so we can enjoy our work, make our art, and love our people.

Begin with Rituals

The nourishing rhythms we incorporate into our days again and again can be used as the building blocks of rituals. A 2017 article "The Psychology of Rituals: An Integrative Review and Process-Based Framework" sums up the role of rituals nicely: "In rituals, the most ordinary of actions and gestures become transformed into symbolic expressions, their meaning reinforced each time they are performed." The authors explain how rituals comprise physical and psychological features that are repeated for enhanced meaning and symbolism, unlike habits, which typically omit requirements for spiritual intimacy or transcendence. "Indeed," they add, "some of our most important rituals would simply appear arbitrary and trivial if the symbolism and meaning were removed. The 21-gun salute during a military funeral service, rather than bestowing the highest honor to a fallen comrade, would be nothing more than group of soldiers firing into the air."[1]

A writer I know posted something on social media several years ago poking fun at those of us who light candles before a writing session. She quipped something along the lines of "just write already. Enough with the rituals and beauty." But rituals—with or without candles—can be helpful. Rituals regulate emotions and motivate people to accomplish specific goals. When performed in a group, rituals increase participants' relational connections with fellow group members, which leads to an enhanced sense of a common purpose, as well as shared social conventions and cultural knowledge among those present. Establishing rituals that help you write on a regular basis will remind you who you are and what you do: you're a writer and you write.

At the end of a spiritual direction session with a writer who was in an especially challenging season of life, I described a few contemplative practices that might help increase her sense of belonging and purpose. One thing I suggested was a simple ritual I've begun doing most mornings: Light a candle. Take six deep breaths with a six-count inhale and a six-count exhale. Read one poem. Blow out the candle. Do the next thing.

If you practice this ritual regularly *in the same spot in your home*, it will provide even more comfort while strengthening your connection to your place and grounding your senses and body to a safe space. If this ritual or a similar one becomes a regular practice, you can turn to it on hard days. The familiar choreography and surroundings will signal to your nervous system that a pause, deep breaths, and verse are imminent with an opportunity to calm down a bit before returning your attention to your difficulties.

Rituals make me happy and settle my soul. They enhance my curiosities and grow my imagination. So, I will continue to tell my family to leave me alone, put my phone on Do Not Disturb, light my manuka honey and bergamot candle, take six deep breaths, and write.

Even if I don't know what to write, I can go through the motions and wait for the next word.

Regular rituals might provide a more secure creative identity and increase your chances of writing more words more often. Too many writers don't have enough time to write. Writers and artists (and everyone else!) have multiple roles. We care for people. We care for our homes. We earn money. We attend church. We develop our craft. We volunteer. We show up for our friends and family and neighbors. We navigate various interruptions and disruptions that require enormous amounts of attention. It's easy to be depleted. It's easy to become exhausted. I see this in myself sometimes. I see it in directees, friends, and colleagues. If rituals can help us put our butts in our chairs to write, the usual obstacles and barriers to the act of writing might begin to crumble.

Poet and cultural critic Hanif Abdurraqib described a beautiful ritual ripe with meaning in a December 2024 Instagram post about his practice of purchasing fresh flowers on a regular basis.

> The Year In Flowers was also one of adapting and transforming rituals. Since late 2020, I've purchased flowers for myself every other week. It is good to have them in the home for beauty's sake, I suppose. But also, as a person who lives with no other human(s,) it's nice to populate my home with things that require me tending to them in order to prolong their life, and, I think, prolong whatever pleasure I can steal out of being alive.
>
> Occupying my brain/hands/heart, even just for a couple of minutes, by urging something beautiful

> towards another day or few hours it wouldn't otherwise have is like building a mirror for my own self/needs/etc.

When preparing for his recent book tour, Abdurraqib sought advice from his more-experienced musician friends. While many shared practical tips about comfort items, one road-worn friend imparted unique wisdom: "They told me to do whatever I needed to do to make sure each day felt different." Abdurraqib implemented this by visiting local florists in every city, collaborating with them to create bouquets that reflected their artistic vision and details he was excited about. These flowers would grace the stage at each reading and appearance. "And for an hour or so, they were my flowers, and then, before I left the stage, I offered them to any people who wanted to come up and grab one. It was my way of reminding myself every day was another day, another occasion for gratitude." Each time Abdurraqib glanced toward the floor, he saw that the day's bouquet was different from all the previous arrangements. "That meant that I'd once again ended up on the good side of a little more stolen time, urged myself towards another day, another few hours."[2]

If Abdurraqib's example inspires you, consider creating a simple ritual that will stimulate your senses when it's time to make some art. Experiment with different easy, doable, *sensory* activities: Light a candle. Make a cup of tea. Put on lip balm. Listen to Beyoncé. Hold some prayer beads. Play with sensory engagement and see which activity or series of activities feels right for your writing practice right now. Try each ritual for a few weeks and see what sticks. On the days you don't feel like writing, tell yourself you're going to at least do your prewriting ritual, then reassess your desire to do more.

Let your rhythms and rituals serve you instead of feeling forced to serve them. If you establish a new ritual to perform before every writing session but then forget about it or go several days without writing, the ritual is still a substantive practice to come back to. It will be waiting for you when you're ready to return to your writing, yourself, your soul.

Begin with Cycles and Spirals

Rhythms and rituals are like magnifying glasses that enhance our vision and enlarge everything in our line of sight, presenting opportunities for deeper participation in natural cyclical patterns. Movements of creativity and spiritual formation follow natural cycles like the periods of sleep and wakefulness that shape our days or the inhales and exhales of the breath that sustains our bodies. These cycles appear throughout our personal lives, relationships, places, seasons in nature, seasons of the church year, and the world beyond our intimate knowledge.

Christina Rossetti often explored the natural world and its seasons to make sense of the spiritual realm. I love Hayley Verdi's beautiful explanation: "The poetry of Christina Rossetti frequently imagines the natural world as a divinely ordered sourcebook for the soul." Verdi stresses that Rossetti's images from nature perform a more substantive role beyond providing a mere metaphor or pastoral setting. "Instead, they are the forms available for the poet to use in her efforts to draw her readers into discerning the theological import of creation."

Since Rossetti wrote hundreds of poems that mention details from God's creation, one can safely assume she gave a large portion of time and attention to noticing what was happening outdoors. Maybe her regular creative process included morning and evening strolls around her garden, quietly contemplating all she saw, and sitting down at her desk for an hour or two to process and respond through the written word.

Verdi's study of Rossetti's first widely read poem collection, *Goblin Market and Other Poems*, shows poetry consistent with "depiction of seasons and their corresponding emotional states . . . and prompt to spiritual understanding and development." Rossetti's poems don't use images from nature to explain various emotional states but use them to set forth the natural world and its seasons of spring, summer, autumn, and winter as a kind of liturgy that evokes particular responses in the reader. *Goblin Market and Other Poems* associates hope, love, and memory with spring, summer, and autumn, respectively, creating seasonal equivalents for these feelings. Across her works, Rossetti explores the spectrum of emotion, especially by casting winter and its associations with coldness and death as a picture of a soul that lacks spiritual capacity. "These consistent emotional associations contribute to her understanding of nature as complementary to the liturgical cycles of the church."

Like many others who make connections between God's creation and God's ways, Rossetti believed God made the natural world, in part to help people have more knowledge of the spiritual realm—that God spoke the world into being to make the unseen seen, the unknowable knowable. Verdi adds that "Rossetti's poetic methods are deeply tied to her belief in the possibilities of the natural world functioning as a 'book' for faithful imaginations to read."[1] We read the natural seasons year after year, again and again, noticing new details and receiving fresh insights as we transition between and reenter the familiarity of spring showers, summer sun, autumn leaves, and winter starkness. Those of us in the church inhabit the liturgical seasons again and again, too. Advent, Christmastide, Epiphany, Lent, Eastertide, and Pentecost invite us into various shapes of the life of Jesus and those he gathers.

While the natural and religious seasons help us gain understanding of the role cycles fulfill, another way to envision this movement is to think of the nautilus, that ancient sea creature whose shell embodies the perfect spiral. As it grows, the nautilus creates new, larger chambers while maintaining the mathematical precision of its spiral shape. Each chamber represents both growth and necessity—the creature must expand to survive, yet it carries the memory of all previous chambers within its form. Writers follow a similar pattern of spiritual and creative growth, building new capacities while carrying forward all we've learned before.

Cycles are an essential component of multiple life experiences. The fundamental rhythms of our creative practice mirror patterns we see

> In nature: Ebb and flow. Rise and recede. Bloom and fade.
> In our bodies: Grasp and release. Contract and expand. Crave and satisfy.
> In our creative work: Generate and refine. Gather and distill. Pick up and put down.

The desolation of winter wakes the brightness of spring. The confusion of creative stagnation opens to the clarity of a realization. Each completion brings us closer to understanding the whole. Spirals, rather than simple circles, better depict this journey because each revolution deepens our comprehension. Like a morning writing session that begins with scattered thoughts but gradually coheres into a poem with a perfect description of the pink Gabriel Oak roses abloom in the front yard, or how returning to a manuscript in January after a busy December full of holiday commitments reveals new layers of meaning. Returning to our writing brings fresh opportunities to see with new eyes and ponder additional connections.

What makes a spiral different from a circle is its dimension of growth—its ability to move not just around but forward or upward or inward, depending on how you're traveling. Sometimes we spiral inward, diving deeper into a particular theme or question in our writing. Other times we spiral outward, expanding our perspective or reaching toward new forms of expression. The path illuminating before us matters as much as the direction—each curve of the spiral offering its own wisdom, its own view of the landscape we're exploring.

In the spiritual life, these spiral patterns reveal themselves through recurring themes and challenges. We might encounter the same spiritual questions about trust or surrender or vocation multiple times throughout our lives, but each encounter finds us changed by previous revolutions of the spiral. What felt like an insurmountable crisis of faith during the season of Lent in our twenties becomes a familiar landscape of questioning during the weeks leading up to Eastertide in our forties—not because the questions are easier, but because we've developed spiritual muscle memory for navigating uncertainty. Like the nautilus's chambers, each spiritual challenge creates space for new growth while building upon the wisdom of past experiences.

The same spiritual lesson—perhaps about patience, or letting go, or trusting divine timing—may appear repeatedly in our lives, but we meet it differently each time. What once triggered resistance might later invite curiosity. What previously led to despair might now prompt reflection. This is the spiral nature of spiritual growth, not a simple circle of repetition, but an ascending path where each turn brings both recognition ("Ah, this Advent lesson on waiting again") and opportunity ("How might I engage it differently this time?").

Our creative practice builds layers of wisdom through cycles of work and rest or presence and absence. The daily practice of showing up to write for fifteen or thirty minutes grows into finished essays over weeks and months. Weekly writing group meetings gradually shape a manuscript. Small rituals of reading and note taking slowly produce larger works. Like the nautilus building its chambers, each small action contributes to the larger pattern of growth.

When you recognize these natural spirals in your creative process, you can work with their inertia rather than against it. This awareness helps you trust the developmental arc of your creativity, even during less generative periods (perhaps like the summer months when days are less structured and predictable schedules are thrown to the wind). Each cycle brings fresh insight while building on what came before, transforming both the work and the writer through every revolution. The spiral pattern reminds us that growth isn't linear—it's a continuous process of expansion and integration, each turn incorporating what came before while creating space for what's yet to emerge. Even during times of difficulty when creative energy wanes, we can meditate on and hope for the various springs of the world and our souls that we know will appear again. Rossetti is an eager companion for this contemplation with her poem "Amen."

Amen

It is over. What is over?
    Nay, how much is over truly:
Harvest days we toiled to sow for;
    Now the sheaves are gathered newly,
    Now the wheat is garnered duly.

It is finished. What is finished?
    Much is finished known or unknown:
Lives are finished; time diminished;
    Was the fallow field left unsown?
    Will these buds be always unblown?

It suffices. What suffices?
    All suffices reckoned rightly:
Spring shall bloom where now the ice is,
    Roses make the bramble sightly,
    And the quickening sun shine brightly,
    And the latter wind blow lightly
And my garden teem with spices.[2]

Begin with More Freedom and Understanding

So much of establishing a sustainable writing practice and having the creative life you want comes down to moving toward a greater sense of freedom and away from anything that squelches and oppresses. Some oppressions are impossible to escape, some aren't, but in my spiritual direction work with writers, I have seen every single person move toward more liberation. Every single one.

If we abide by the rules someone else has created to determine what it means to be a writer—or a person—we reinforce the status quo. It's important to assess why you do what you do. Do you have to do it the way everyone else does it? Is there a more creative way to do the thing you want to do (write more, rest more, have a different day job or weekend schedule so you can write and rest more) instead of going with a flow that's carrying you to a destination you'd rather not visit? Reclaiming your agency regarding your time and energy provides entryways to vaster and more nurturing landscapes from which to create and make your art.

Relinquishing the need to conform to external standards opens you up to the full spectrum of your unique experiences of life. It's from this place of authenticity that your writing will find its true voice and resonance. Maybe you'll discover different ways to honor your writerly self while increasing the amount of joy and delight in your creative process and receiving more nourishment overall.

Writers, of course, have inherited lots of scripts about what writers "should" do—but these scripts can be set aside. Perhaps you prefer to write at noon, instead of rising to get to the desk as the birds wake. Maybe you choose to write in short bursts throughout the day rather than forcing yourself into long, uninterrupted sessions. Maybe you prefer simple solo writing retreats even though some insist that "real writers" must apply for and attend competitive workshops and residencies.

Freedom in writing practice isn't about abandoning all structure—it's about knowing which structures serve *your* preferences and creative spirit. The right frameworks enable growth rather than constraining it much like a proper trellis supports a climbing vine. This might mean creating unconventional writing rituals, finding unexpected times for creativity, or developing your own metrics for progress that have nothing to do with word counts or publication credits.

Understanding grows alongside this freedom as we release external pressures and expectations. We begin to recognize our natural creative rhythms and honor our preferred processes. We also become more trusting of our intuition for what our soul and writing need, and with this deeper self-knowledge we write not from obligation but from desire and enjoyment.

Twelve years after the session in which my therapist told me to write more, I reached out to Julie to see if she could meet with me. I wanted to know if she remembered giving me her pivotal advice. This was our first conversation in several years, and it was comfortable and familiar to be in her presence again. She had zero recollection of telling me to write and shook her head no in response to the few follow-up questions I asked in between sips of her tea. But what she told me next was huge: "The only reason I would've told you to write more was because I knew you were a writer and that you weren't living into the fullness of that identity. I would never tell every therapy client to write more, but I will always tell writers to write more." How good it is to be seen and known. Perhaps that's another way to begin—to see and know our writerly selves with more clarity and greater understanding.

Belong

You are
such an
interesting conversation.
You belong
here.

—Pádraig Ó Tuama

To belong is to find your place in the vast web of connection that sustains creative life. Just as birds know their migration paths or roots find water underground, writerly belonging is both instinct and intention, both gift and practice.

Writers belong first to themselves. You belong to your authentic voice, your natural rhythms, your unique way of seeing the world. This self-belonging creates a foundation for all other connections. When you write, you belong more fully to who you are and who you're becoming. Writing helps you be more of who you were made to be.

We belong to our writing spaces—the desk by the window, the kitchen stool at the island, the favorite chair in the living room, the café where words flow easily. And we belong to our rituals—the morning pages, the afternoon walks, the evening reading. These physical anchors and repetitive actions ground us in the writing life and establish homes for our creativity to dwell.

Writers belong to each other, too. In writing groups and workshops, we find our kindred spirits. Those who understand the struggle with the blank page, the joy of a sentence that sings, the necessity of showing up again and again to the work.

To belong is to be "at hand, together with." We are present to ourselves, to others, to the divine, to our places, to the world. It's finding our narrative in the great conversation of literature while adding our voice to the chorus of those who write to understand and make meaning.

Belonging happens gradually, naturally, surprisingly. And belonging can also happen in an instant, take work, and be unsurprising. Sometimes through writing itself, the way words on a page help us make sense of the broader world. Sometimes through community, the way other writers reflect to us our own truth. Always through practice and continuing to show up to that which calls us to create.

Belong to Yourself

How we approach our writing life matters because we're not our fullest selves when we're not writing. When discussing belonging with writers, one topic that comes up regularly is identity. "How secure are you in your writerly identity?" and "how does writing help you belong to yourself?" are two questions I might ask during a session, and I welcome you to reflect on those questions now. Each time you consider your responses, you bring new experiences and understanding, inviting deeper insights.

It's tempting to think religion, politics, and other social dynamics that can divide us from one another are more powerful than the humanity that unifies us. Narratives of division are an unending waterfall, the sound of which reverberates from news outlets, social media, Sunday school, and Thanksgiving gatherings with extended family. These days I'm more concerned with remembering all our belongings because I don't want to lose sight of our deepest, most abiding connections—*and* because I *do* wish to feel that keener, quicker sense of belonging with the people, places, and parts of myself with whom I feel most at home.

Writers belong first to ourselves when we put words on the page. Each time we write, we strengthen our connection to our authentic voice and deepen our understanding of our inner landscape. Discovering new aspects of who we are increases our curiosity about who we are becoming. We can grow our sense of belonging through the writing process regardless of the existence or absence of loneliness.

My own journey with belonging began early. An isolating experience at a YMCA day camp the summer before I entered kindergarten remains the first scene in my personal film of disconnection. Years later, when I wrote about that young girl, standing alone on the playground while other children played together, I saw something crucial about the relationship between writing and belonging. The act of writing created a kind of belonging—not just to a community of other people who shared similar experiences, but also to myself, even my past self.

But writing's power to help us belong to ourselves extends far beyond processing difficult experiences. When we write, we expand our ability to fully inhabit our thoughts while exploring our curiosities and honoring our natural rhythms. This self-belonging emerges through writerly activities: crafting sentences that capture exactly what we mean, discovering unexpected metaphors that illuminate our understanding, or simply showing up to the page day after day to see what might happen next.

Think of the writer who rises early and immediately begins her morning pages, because those predawn stream-of-conscious journaling sessions reveal her own voice amid the noise of daily life. Or consider the poet who carries a notebook everywhere, jotting down observations and fragments of language, belonging more fully to his way of seeing the world with each entry. These practices help us dwell within ourselves more completely.

Writing also hands us opportunities to discover and establish our own unique creative rhythms, which can be a sort of secret we keep with our soul. Some of us write in bursts of imagination and energy, while others maintain steady daily practices. Some need long stretches of solitude to produce work, while others thrive on short, frequent encounters with the page. As we write, we learn to trust these natural peaks and flatter terrains, belonging more fully to our unique creativity.

This self-belonging through writing manifests in more concrete ways, too. It shows up when you choose words that precisely match your meaning, as you develop your distinctive voice and style, through exploring the topics and themes you return to again and again, in your preferred times and spaces for writing, and through the genres and forms that feel most natural to you. The more you write, the more you discover about yourself as a writer. You learn the contours of your values, questions, obsessions, and preferred ways of making meaning. Writing becomes a familiar home we can return to, regardless of what's going on outside and around the home.

Belong to God

Writers discern holy presence in countless ways. Creative work can be a form of prayer or meditation, connecting us to the divine in quiet moments of writing, in our struggles with blank pages, and in the vulnerability of sharing one's work. Writers can find belonging in the sacred corners of the creative process where God meets them in their imaginative expression and in the rituals associated with a regular writing practice. This belonging to the divine happens through embracing both the grace of seclusion and the grace of community. The solitude necessary for work becomes holy ground, while connections with other writers, spiritual companions, artful encounters, and favorite places become anchoring points that make writing and faith richer, more layered, less lonely.

Brian Doyle's experience of fatherhood powerfully illustrates one way writing and divine belonging can intersect: Writing can be a response to the sense of divine gift. When Doyle's son Liam was born with a heart containing three chambers instead of four, the family faced two harrowing open-heart surgeries before their son's second birthday. Years later, with Liam thriving at age nine, Doyle wrote *Wet Engine: Exploring the Mad Wild Miracle of the Heart* as what he called "a sort of prayer of thanks" for his son's life. In the book's introduction, Doyle shares three truths he had discovered: "One: stories matter waaaaay more than we know. Two: all stories are, in some form, prayers. Three: love is the story and the prayer that matters the most."[1]

For other writers, the persistent questioning that creative work entails is a way of attending to the holy in their midst. During a recent public event with André Holland and Imani Perry celebrating Perry's book *Black in Blues: How a Color Tells the Story of My People*, a member of the audience asked what role faith plays in their art. Perry responded first without hesitating: "It's all over the place. It's expansive. My spiritual landscape is very broad and complex but it's in everything."[2]

When I had a moment to ask a follow-up question during my turn at the book-signing table, I asked Perry if she could share more about how the act of writing is a spiritual practice. "Sometimes it's like prayer," she told me. "Other times it's more of an interrogation."

After I got home with my signed copy, I sank into a corner of the sofa and looked for Perry's interrogations. The first sentence of the book is a question. "Which is your favorite color blue?" she asks her cousin's son while they are sitting in her grandmother's bedroom full of many shades of blue. More questions follow not far behind—just a few paragraphs down and onto the next page:

> My blue begins here inside her-our-my home. The walls, the shaggy rug, the printed birds that were once perched inside an artificial wood frame by the window, the cotton covers and blue-inked words of prayer on paper tucked in the corner of her vanity.

> What led her to all that blue? Was it the parade of wildflowers of Alabama: the bluebells, mouse-ears, chicory, bluets, wild hyacinth, dayflowers, aster, or toadflax, and their curving, springing, luscious blues? Was it just our sky, crisp and divine? Was she inspired by her youth in the country, where having the blues lent passion to the sound of gospel in Sunday morning baptismal waters and mixed with amber liquids and guitars after dark?[3]

The questions thread throughout the book, exploring the significance of blue in Black life and culture: "Why so much blue? And what makes it matter? What makes it mournful and hopeful and Black?" These questions probe deeply into spiritual practices, like the bottle trees hung with blue glass in crepe myrtles—a tradition with roots in Kongo culture that speaks to protecting vulnerable souls. Writing about broken pottery found at Saint Croix's sugar plantations, Perry contemplates the painful history embedded in the clay fragments: shards of dishes that broke naturally, were ceremonially smashed, or shattered in rebellion. These artifacts ask Perry (and her readers) to consider whose ancestors held these crocks and jugs and candlesticks, whose blood was shed by them, and how these broken vessels speak stories that can never be made whole.[4] Perry's questions represent a way of belonging to the divine through persistent wondering. I picture the spaces around Perry's spiritual wanderings as expansive pastures extending beyond any horizon. Each question has plenty of room to roam and become what it needs to be for Perry and her stories.

The act of writing can be a form of contemplative practice, in which the blank page exists as a space for divine encounter. Melissa Febos writes that, for her, art "is a form of worship, a medicine, a solitary and a social act." She goes on, "It is an ancient process through which I draw closer to my ancestors." She then describes how writing helps her experience the divine: "On the page, I undergo a change of heart, I return to the past and make something new from it, I forgive myself and am freed from old harms, I return to love and am blessed with more than enough to give away. Every single thing I have created worth a damn has been a practice of love, healing, and redemption. I know this process to be divine."[5]

Whether we're crafting fiction, poetry, or personal essays, each word written with intention can become a kind of prayer. Writers might feel compelled to approach their craft as a form of devotion, finding God's presence in both the struggle and the flow of creative expression. As you explore how writing helps you belong to the divine, expand your vision toward other areas of life. Notice how prayerful or meditative writing deepens your sense of self while opening your heart to others. Let your questions about creativity and connection become invitations to deeper dialogue with the sacred, trusting that every honest word written is a step toward more authentic belonging.

Belong to Your Body

Honoring our bodies is another way we as writers can belong to ourselves and the divine. Over the years, I've noticed many writers ignore their physical pain, their exhaustion, and other messages from their body. So much of the writing process relies on our minds and ideas; we can get stuck there like we're riding an intellectual merry-go-round, convinced that we're having fun. And maybe it is fun at first. But we're too distracted by the music, atmosphere, and the pressure to enjoy ourselves to notice how uncomfortable it is to sit atop the carved horse or elephant or giraffe. Our bodies are rarely our priority.

While everyone's relationship with and responses to their bodies are complex, I agree with Tricia Hersey—that grind culture, "a collaboration between capitalism and white supremacy," is the primary reason we neglect our bodies.[1] The seemingly constant pressure to do more, work more, prove more and more and more has all kinds of negative effects on us. But the oppression of grind culture isn't the only reason we sometimes check out of our bodies. Sometimes we'd rather work and play and create instead of scheduling and showing up for an annual mammogram or eye exam. I forget my body because I've fallen down the rabbit hole of researching the history of elementary education in Alabama and want to keep reading instead of making time for a wholesome meal. Or, you might forget your body and ignore your aching knees while attending your artist friend's gallery opening because you love her and believe her art is important. Or, you skip your dentist appointment because a work project took more time than you anticipated, and it's been way too long since you visited your father who lives two states away and you really need to get on the road now instead of getting your teeth cleaned.

So many reasons for forgetting! Yet, it's crucial to take account of our bodies. How can you remember your hands, feet, skin, bones, and every cell that forms your physical being? How can you practice not forgetting?

During a recent conversation with a writer who lives with debilitating chronic pain, I offered the language of belonging to invite more creative curiosity in her responses to her bodily suffering. I asked: "How can you belong to different portions of your full self?" Given her physical discomfort and exhaustion, I opened up the question's frame to include not just her body but her *self*, to give her some extra space. How can her body belong to her mind? How can her emotions belong to her soul? After a pause, she said she hadn't thought much about how she belongs in these deconstructed ways. She proceeded to explore the following questions: If her physical needs are at their peak, how can her mind pause while the body receives more of what it needs? What would it look like for heart and soul to give preferential treatment to what this more needy member of the full unit currently requires? In what ways can she tweak her writing commitments to mitigate her body's disruptions?

This paradigm shift encourages more intentional self-awareness and establishes greater connections between the pieces of us that form the whole. We will have more understanding of another idea from Hersey in *Rest Is Resistance*. We will view "our bodies as a miracle, and a place of reverence" and know "we are blessed to have a body, to be chosen to be alive, to breathe, to make choices, and to proclaim that our bodies are our own."[2]

If you're thinking, "All of this sounds lovely, but I don't have much bandwidth for such things. I'd rather give extra time to writing instead of the intricacies of my body's belongings"—okay. I hear you. But consider this: Your body is your first and most intimate writing partner. It holds your memories, carries your experiences, and shapes how you perceive the world. When we ignore our bodies, we cut ourselves off from a vital source of creative wisdom. The tension in your shoulders might be telling you something about your character's anxiety. The way your breath changes when you write about certain topics could reveal deeper truths about your subject matter.

Start with breath, then turn your attention to your body. Where do you notice imbalance, pain, tension, energy? This simple practice can ground you in your physical experience before writing.

In *Strong like Water*, Aundi Kolber suggests developing a "somatic vocabulary" to help tune into and describe bodily sensations. This practice serves writers doubly: it helps us connect with our own bodies, and it enriches our ability to write about physical experience. Kolber offers words like "achy," "buzzy," "expansive," "radiating," "saturated," and "tingly" as starting points for describing bodily sensations.[3] Notice which words resonate with your current physical state. Which might work for describing a character's embodied experience? Which spur your curiosity?

Take a few minutes to explore these sensations in your journal. Add your own words to describe how your body feels. This isn't just an exercise in self-awareness—it's building a vocabulary for more vivid, embodied writing. Remember: Your creativity doesn't live in your head alone—it pulses through every cell of your being. Belonging to our bodies isn't another item on our to-do list; it's an invitation to greater integration and attentive writing from our whole selves.

Belong to Your Desires

One writer I met with felt terrible about wanting her first book to sell more copies and garner more attention than it did. She was wrestling with complicated feelings about the stresses and disappointments of the publishing process. Hefty doses of guilt and shame made everything else heavier, and she wondered if she should quit writing altogether. "Maybe I'm just not cut out for this."

Her feelings of failure and frustration felt like too much for her to hold. She had even convinced herself that her lack of contentment with the book's publication was proof that she was a bad Christian. Her shame about the disappointment itself was preventing her from truly acknowledging her sadness and moving on to other creative endeavors. She attempted to process all of it, but nothing seemed to help her move through the hard feelings about her book and her identity as a writer.

It's normal for an author to want her book to sell well. I would be worried about any writer who doesn't care if anyone ever reads what they write. But few books are best sellers, so most authors experience disappointment over their sales. And even those who have a breakout book often end up wanting more. It's human nature to rarely be satisfied, so it behooves all of us to practice navigating the terrain of desire and unsatisfaction.

Desiring good things for ourselves and for others is not wrong. But the good things we want for our writing—our hope to get a book deal or to have a poem accepted by a dream magazine—are never the only things we want. Our writerly desires are not our sole desires.

I shared a mental exercise with my disappointed writer that Lauren Winner first shared with me a few years ago: ordering our desires. Find your favorite pen and a notebook and settle into a comfortable spot and put some thought into creating a list of your top ten desires. Then rank them in order of importance. Signing a two-book contract and having a breakout best seller might be on your list. Where do they fall? Are they your most desired desires? Again, publishing success is a normal thing for a writer to want—but writers finally have very little control over the market success of their books. Can you reorder your list so that "have a sustainable writing life" and "enjoy the writing process regardless of recognition" edge out "glowing review in the *New York Times*"?

After hearing about this process of ordering desires, the debut author's eyes brightened. She might've even smiled. She told me her top spots would go to loving God and loving people. Then wanting her family and friends and herself to flourish. Wanting members of her community to be safe. She was so relieved when she realized it was okay to want her book to do well because she wants other things, too. Recognizing our non-publishing-related desires will smooth some of the rough patches on the road to greater satisfaction.

But our desires are not static. Our longings will shift and turn. They may become disordered during emotional dips, exhaustion peaks, worsening circumstances, or power cravings. When my desire for my book to do well displaces all my other wants, I notice that my writing energy changes (usually, though not always, for the worse), my social media presence changes (always for the worse), my inner dialogue changes. It happens. It's something for me to pay attention to. It's also a sign that it's time to pause and give additional thought to what caused the disorder. I know what I need to do to get my writerly desires in their proper place. Do you? Here's something to consider: Maybe you need to want more, not less. Maybe you need to make a new list of your top ten hopes. Maybe you need to name a few desires that have been hiding in silence.

Belong to Time

Sometimes shifting directions toward more of what you want is overwhelming. Experimenting with ways to be more nourished and less depleted sounds like a good idea, but isn't it just one more thing to do on a list that's already too long? You look up from your calendar and see obligations and responsibilities hovering like low-lying clouds threatening to wash away any desires and plans you might make for flourishing. Taking time to slow down and consider how to properly care for yourself may seem like an option that only increases your risk of becoming soaked to the bone when the rain eventually falls. Who has time to deal with that wet mess?

But what if this is another opportunity to start small and simple? Let's return to the idea of writing for shorter-than-preferred periods of time that we explored in the previous chapter. What if, in addition to helping you establish a new writing practice, devoting smaller chunks of time to your creativity and other nourishing rhythms can improve how you inhabit all of time? While "Begin with Fifteen Minutes" focused on starting a practice, belonging to time involves developing a more intimate relationship with how we move through our days. Just as spiritual practices can ground us in the now, short writing sessions can become doorways to deeper presence. When we tune in to our inner world and write for just ten or fifteen minutes, we're opening ourselves to short bursts of contemplation. Thomas Merton wrote that we might arrive at this state "by an intuitive awakening in which our free and personal reality becomes fully alive to its own existential depths, which open out into the mystery of God."[1] When we ignore everything else and give our attention to the landscape of our heart, soul, and mind, we claim these moments as sacred, regardless of their brevity.

This belonging to time extends beyond the writing itself. When we honor these smaller pockets of creativity—a quick morning journal entry, a brief revision session between meetings, a few moments of free writing or note-taking before bed—we begin to see all of time differently. Time changes from something to battle against into a space fertile with possibility. Rather than viewing time as a scarce resource to manage, we can experience it as a generous companion in our creative journey.

Consider how different writers have belonged to their particular moments: Emily Dickinson writing at her small desk late into the night, Virginia Woolf claiming her "room of one's own" during afternoon sessions, Toni Morrison writing in the early morning darkness before her children awoke.[2] Each found their way of belonging to time while honoring their life's unique rhythms. Their examples remind us that there's no single "right" way to belong to time—only the way that aligns with our own seasons and circumstances.

While short writing sessions move us toward our goals, they also teach us to belong more fully to our days. When we become friends with the smaller spaces between larger commitments, we develop what some contemplatives call "sacred awareness"—the ability to see divine presence in all moments, not just the ones marked for spiritual practice. This friendship with time allows us to notice and accept invitations we might otherwise miss: the quiet morning that beckons us to write, the unexpected cancellation that offers a window for creativity, the evening lull that invites reflection.

Developing your friendship with time can extend beyond these moments of awareness into practical shifts in how you structure your days. Adjusting regular routines is one way to create more space for writing. Could your weekly grocery run become fortnightly, freeing up additional writing sessions each month? Could certain tasks be batched or streamlined to protect creative time? More importantly, can you search for examples of how time manifests as abundance rather than scarcity? Look for evidence of time's gifts: stacks of books you've read, houseplants with new growth, an heirloom quilt folded atop a chest. These tangible reminders show us that the passage of time doesn't always represent a depletion or a running out of—it can also represent accumulation: of stories, of growth, of wisdom and warmth passed through generations. As we shift our perspective from viewing time as an adversary to seeing it as an ally, we experience less tension and more connection. We begin to trust time's rhythms, finding our place within its natural flow rather than constantly fighting against it.

Belong to the Liturgical Year

There is a December I carry with me—full of Advent longing and ache, skirted by the hope that swells even when the heart is tired of waiting. Years ago, when I was wrestling with infertility, I sat in a darkened church each week and watched a different family light the Advent candles. My gaze followed the children's restlessness and the parents' fullness while my own emptiness felt like a scream in the hush. I believed Emmanuel had come, and would come again, but I didn't know if my own longing—to mother, to belong to my body—would ever be fulfilled. My faith didn't erase that loneliness; it bore witness.

Many writers know such longing. The unfinished story; the unfulfilled manuscript; the sense of being on the edge of a community, not quite inside. What comfort I've found is not a cure for loneliness but an anchor—a reminder that my story, personal and creative, is stitched into a narrative far larger than myself. The liturgical year, in its slow, spiraling rhythm, offers to writers the same invitation it extends to all the faithful: to locate ourselves in a story of anticipation, lament, hope, and communion.

"The Christian year, by its rhythms, allows us an opportunity both to look back and remember the story of Christ, and to look forward to its ultimate conclusion,"

Bobby Gross reminds us.[1] For me, and perhaps for you, too, these rhythms of the church year and other cycles aren't about escaping what is difficult or diminishing what feels unfinished. Instead, they are a way to mark time as writers—each season welcoming us anew into practices of waiting, mourning, celebrating, and remembering. Our writing, too, benefits from seasons. Advent's waiting might prompt us to rest with greater curiosity before a blank page. Lent's introspection can challenge us to tell bold truths and express honest lament. Each period in the church year is an entry point for creative ritual.

Observing the church year teaches us that our lives are not linear but cyclical; this is also wisdom for writers, whose creative paths rarely unfold in a tidy manner. The turning of seasons invites us to revisit past creative efforts, to reflect on what has changed, grown, or needs tending. Each period of fasting or feasting holds memories of who I was in seasons past as well as who I am in the present. Doubts on doubts, starts and stops, the essays I offered once in vulnerability while trying to hope for hope. When I pull out the bright red tablecloth for Pentecost, its ritual is both household and spiritual, but these days I find myself considering: What could it look like to mark my writing seasons as tangibly? What objects and actions might help me remember and anticipate as a writer, too? How might the flame and fire of Pentecost light my writerly way?

Even in the cycles of belonging, loneliness may persist. Loss and isolation—familiar companions for writers—are not always swept away by ritual or the passage of time. But the liturgical year, like the writing life, promises that we are not abandoned to our own stories. On the days when I cannot celebrate, when words evade me or community feels far off, I remember the generations who have kept vigil, who wrote anyway, and waited for the light to break again. Their witness helps me write my way back through the shadows toward communion with God, with others, with my own vocation.

This past Advent, as the morning bloomed into its first purple glow, I wrote "First Sunday of Advent" at the top of the first page of a blank journal. This small gesture—using a new journal at the beginning of each new church year—has become its own ritual, my annual entry into expectant waiting, both in spirit and in the creative work that follows. Each liturgical turn asks me (and perhaps you, too): What will I remember this season? How might I write anew the stories that bind me to the sacred and the ordinary?

As I enter a season of the church calendar, I anticipate another opportunity for familiar rituals—readings, prayers, practices, written words—that will bring me closer to myself, to community, to God, and to my craft. The liturgical year, like our creative lives, invites us to belong again.

Belong to a Literary Community

Generations of writers have gathered for creative inspiration and moral support. Virginia Woolf's modernist prose echoes the artistic techniques of her painter friends who rejected traditional forms and focused more on subjective experience and fragmentation.[1] Woolf and the painters with whom she gathered may have shaped not just one another's form and style but also their content: a picture painted by Vanessa Bell, Woolf's sister and fellow member of the Bloomsbury group, was given to Woolf just before she began to write *Mrs. Dalloway*. It shows glamorous guests at a party much like the occasion Woolf depicted in her novel.[2] Another example includes how the Lost Generation's passionate arguments were formational for Ernest Hemingway's *The Sun Also Rises* and F. Scott Fitzgerald's *The Great Gatsby*. And during meetings of The Inklings, J. R. R. Tolkien shared early drafts of *The Lord of the Rings*, while C. S. Lewis refined *The Screwtape Letters* over pipes and pints. In the 1930s, the South Side Writers Group brought together Richard Wright, Margaret Walker, and Frank Marshall Davis for discussions from which Wright's *Native Son* and Walker's *For My People* emerged.

Margaret Walker describes the first time she went to the South Side Writers Group in Chicago: "Twice I left the house and turned back, the first time out of great self-consciousness because I felt I looked abominable. I had nothing to wear to make a nice appearance, and I was going to the far South Side, where I felt people would make fun of me. But my great desire to meet writers and end my long isolation conquered this superficial fear. I made myself go."[3]

According to Robert Luckett, director of the Margaret Walker Center, the South Side Writers Group was more vital than a casual gathering and source for creative inspiration. Luckett explained, "Life was hard for Margaret in her early years in Chicago. She continued to face discrimination, especially at Northwestern, and was broke most of the time." Luckett thinks she was likely depressed. "Richard Wright and the South Side Writers gave her a community that helped her find her worth in the world, even if her relationship with Wright burned hotly for a minute before fizzling out."[4] Her courage to overcome initial hesitation led to lasting connections that nurtured both her work and her spirit—a pattern that continues to play out in writing friendships and communities today.

Relationships in literary communities grow through repeated encounters. Each interaction adds another layer of trust and mutual support. While it may be challenging to plant the first seeds of writerly friendship, the spiral nature of relationship building means that each additional genuine connection creates momentum for deeper bonds and future encounters. Like a garden that becomes more established each season, writing friendships develop their own sustainable rhythms of giving and receiving.

Being part of a literary community transforms the solitary act of writing into a collaborative journey of growth. Beyond the practical benefits of feedback and accountability, writing groups provide fertile soil where both relationships and craft can flourish. These connections often yield fruit through shared learning, new opportunities, or the gift of trusted readers who understand both your work and your vision.

The friendship between Danté Stewart and Nefertiti Robinson demonstrates how literary relationships spiral deeper through shared experiences. Their connection, which began in a church community, has grown through cycles of joy and suffering, bringing them closer to their authentic voices as writers. Robinson expressed gratitude for how Stewart articulates their community's experiences: "It has been so incredible to watch the world have experiences, have our responses to those experiences, and then see our responses translated and put into the world in a format that speaks very well for our community."

The most transformative season of their friendship emerged through shared suffering—losing their church family while navigating racial trauma and new parenthood. Like winter yielding to spring, this difficult period forged a vibrant connection. Robinson described how this season forced them to "find a way to survive our time" and "figure out a way" to maintain hope.

Their literary friendship continues to expand, enriching not just their own work but their broader community. As Stewart noted, "Me and Nef have been on this continual journey of reading the literature, reading the books, trying to study the tradition, trying to be in the tradition." Their literary friendship has continually renewed, forming ever-widening paths toward creative growth and mutual support.[5]

May this cyclical approach to literary friendship become one of the rhythms of our lives—where we grow together through times of abundance and scarcity, each turn of the spiral bringing us closer to our authentic voices and shared creative vision.

Belong to Traditions

Writers belong not just to our present-day communities but to the long lineage of those whose souls have worked with words before us. We have inherited techniques, insights, and ways of seeing from those who have shaped language into meaning for generations before we were born. Poet Scott Cairns reminds us that literature is a conversation: "Virtually every work written over the centuries has been to some degree a responsive text, something of an epistolary response to what the writer beholds—the landscape, the heavens, or—as in most cases—another prior text."[1] Cairns expands on this idea in an interview about his book *Correspondence with My Greeks*: "Original writing is writing that bears the marks of its origins. . . . Authentic work carries the imprint of the tradition that shaped it, even as it becomes something new."[2]

Belonging to a literary tradition is a bit like belonging to a faith tradition—as a Christian, I don't invent my life with God from whole cloth but receive the wisdom and practices and insights (as well as the burdens and damage) of the generations before. Writers enter our traditions through practice, through working and reworking language until it shapes us as much as we shape it.

During spiritual direction sessions, writers often express anxiety about finding their place within literary and spiritual traditions. They worry about originality or whether they have any new ideas to contribute. But belonging to a tradition is neither about mimicking what's come before nor about wholly innovating—it's about entering existing conversations with the full self—all of one's remembering and all of one's experiences. Like liturgy that becomes "endless" through practice, our relationship with literary and faith traditions deepens through engagement. Each time we read deeply, write honestly, or revise carefully, we participate in this ongoing dialogue. Each time we sit in silence, meditate, pray, or notice the presence of the divine, we participate in this intimate exchange.

Jesmyn Ward's *Let Us Descend* offers a striking example of this dynamic. In her novel, Ward reshapes Dante's *Inferno* to confront the infernos of American slavery.[3] The protagonist, Annis, descends not into a mythological underworld but into the hellscape of the antebellum South.[4] Ward borrows Dante's structure of layered suffering but fills it with the voices of enslaved ancestors, Yoruba spiritual guides, and the grief of a stolen lineage. She doesn't merely retell the *Inferno*; she reclaims it. By stitching her story onto Dante's fabric, Ward honors the tradition while subverting its Eurocentric roots, proving that even ancient forms can carry urgent, untold stories.[5]

Ward's act of literary belonging is both homage and rebellion. She writes into the conversation Cairns describes—responding to Dante's medieval Christian vision with her own Black southern spirituality. Her novel bears the "handprints" of its origins, yet it becomes something wholly new. This is tradition as a living force: not a monument to the dead, but a forge where inherited tools reshape raw pain into art.

Belonging to a tradition, then, is an act of sacred tension. Like Ward, we might dismantle a canonical structure to build shelter for those who have suffered. Or like Cairns, we might press ancient Greek terms into service for modern spiritual inquiry. Tradition is a loom. Writers inherit its threads, but we choose the patterns. We decide what to unravel, what to mend, and what new colors to weave into the textile.

This is why the anxiety of influence fades when we realize that we are not latecomers to the conversation. We're its next breath. Every act of writing—whether revising a poem or reimagining an epic—says to the tradition: "I heard you. Now let me show you what I've seen."

Belong to a Poem

Even for those of us who are principally writers of prose, poetry can be a key part of a nourishing life and writing practice. Poetry expands creativity, faith, and the ability to inhabit this world. By providing words, images, metaphors, empty space, truncated lines, and pauses of all kinds, poems are bells that ring true for our inner worlds and reverberate throughout our experiences in more external realms. Favorite poems make it easier to face whatever any day may bring. In many ways that are full of mystery and unknowable, poetry helps us feel more like humans who deserve to be our full selves in a world that often obsesses over who's in and who's out.

I've been fortunate to ask a few poets how poetry has saved them and helped them belong. The responses from two such interactions follow.

How Poetry Saved Ashley M. Jones

Ashley Jones describes her experience like this:

"Poetry made me feel like I belong here. And here means a lot of different places. Here on earth, here in Alabama, here in my Black body. I think the poets who instruct me like Lucille Clifton, Gwendolyn Brooks, Nabila Lovelace—those people kind of let me know that I could enter the room. And again, the room is many places. It's the planet. I could enter the planet and I feel I belong. I could enter my Blackness and feel like it was enough.

"Because growing up, I wasn't always sure that I really belonged. As I said before, I'm a weird person and people always say, 'You're not weird,' but I know that I am. I'm a poet, so there's some inherent weirdness there, which I don't mean negatively. I see the world like a poet sees the world, which is just a different way.

"But being in Alabama and being a Black person who's not affiliated with the church was definitely something that made me feel unusual. Being someone who was really into books and imagination, and I don't know, I just was a weird kid. I always was like, 'How can I fit in? I love being Black. How do I be Black and be me at the same time? I don't sound like my grandma. I don't sound like my mom. I don't sound like whoever, but I still want to be invited in.'

"And so, I found these poems. I always tell the story of the moment I decided that I wanted to be a poet, which was reciting the poem "Harriet Tubman" by Eloise Greenfield in the second grade. When that poem left my mouth, I finally heard myself as a Black woman—or a Black girl at that point. I saw myself belonging, finally.

"Even though my poems don't sound like that poem, I feel I'm doing the same thing. I'm making space for people to feel like they belong."

How Poetry Saved Kaveh Akbar

Kaveh Akbar's background is very different from Ashley's, but poetry similarly shapes his writing:

"I was born in Iran and came to America as a young child. When we came to America, my parents banned speaking Farsi in the household. My brother is seven years older than me, so he was in school. He was struggling in school because he's coming from Farsi-speaking schools, immediately into English-speaking schools, with no ESL programs like they have today or anything like that. And he was really struggling. So, my parents, and I mean, you can understand why they would do it, banned speaking Farsi in the household, but consequentially, we lost our Farsi. And so, I don't speak my first language.

"I've taken classes over the years and gotten tutors and stuff, but I don't really speak my first language anymore. So I have spent my whole life separated from the country and people with which I was born. I've never been in a class with another Iranian, let alone a classroom full of Iranians. In a room full of Iranians, I feel like the least Iranian person, because I left when I was a kid and I don't really speak the language fluently. In a room full of Americans, I've certainly never felt American. That's a lot of separateness. There's a lot of separateness that I feel. But in poems I find amongness.

"I remember when I was a kid, it used to trip me out that when I was sad, I would want to listen to sad music. It kind of stands to reason that when you're sad, you would want to listen to Weird Owl or the Berenstain Bears, or some goofy, happy stuff or whatever. But whenever I was sad, I just wanted to listen to sad-sack ballads and this sort of thing. And I wondered if that was some weird masochistic streak in me, but I think what it was and what it is, is that when I was sad and when I am sad, I want to hear someone else be like, 'Yeah, I was sad too. And I lived to sing about it.'

"I think that's the sort of amongness that poetry gives me. The fortitude that poetry gives me is the amongness of the resilient, the amongness of those who persevered long enough to write. And it's a profound privilege to get to add my little whispers into those conversations that have preceded me by millennia. To get to whisper into that conversation is the bedrock privilege upon which I've built my life."[1]

If you want to do a close reading of a poem and determine if poetry can save you, try this: Take six deep breaths with a six-count inhale and a six-count exhale, then read one of the poems that follow. Then read it again, aloud this time. Read it once again. Then journal or write a letter to a friend about how this poem helps you feel less alone, how it helps you belong to yourself, others, the divine, and the world. Then see what happens next.

God Made My Whole Body

By Ashley M. Jones

and the way it moves, and the way it shakes and jiggles and plops, and
God made my smile and the thousand tears that fall from my eyes,
God made the sun and the moon and the leaf held loosely in my
godson's perfect little hand, and God made the summer breeze and
the guitar Ron Isley crooned over, and God made the grass and the
bugs and the dogs and the trees, and God made all of our bodies to

make waste, and God made even the waste that lives in us, and God made the way the world spins and the way it will shake us right off if we don't act right, and God made the rivers which make it possible for us to drink, and God made the clouds which hold the rain, and God made the birds which fly and the wolves that howl. God made the folds of my brain and the thoughts that burrow there. God made my belly, my uterus and all the little eggs which might become children—God made the doubt that rests there, like bubbling gas. God made the silence I wrap around myself some nights, alone. God made the music we sing and the music we hate. God made the ears which help us stay balanced, help us to hear what people say behind our backs and in front of them. God made sweet potato pie and aunties and mamas who know how to add just enough nutmeg. God made my whole body. And God made my grandma and her gold tooth, and God made my grandma and her curly wig, and God made my grandma I didn't know, and God made my grandpa who was a ghost, and my grandpa who was a terror. God made fear and the way it slices us up thin and flimsy, God made the way a hand quivers before it strikes. God made pain. God made the blood which runs and keeps us running. God made an everlasting red.[2]

How Prayer Works
By Kaveh Akbar

Tucked away in our tiny bedroom so near each other the
edge of my prayer rug covered the edge of his, my brother
and I prayed. We were 18 and 11 maybe, or 19 and 12. He
was back from college where he built his own computer
and girls kissed him on the mouth. I was barely anything,
just wanted to be left alone to read and watch *The Simpsons*.

We prayed together as we had done thousands of times,
rushing ablutions over the sink, laying our janamazes
out toward the window facing the elm which one sum-
mer held an actual crow's nest full of baby crows: fuzzy,
black-beaked fruit, they were miracles we did not think to
treasure.

My brother and I hurried through sloppy postures of
praise, quiet as the light pooling around us. The room
was so small the twin bed took up nearly all of it, and
as my brother, tall and endless, moved to kneel, his foot
caught the coiled brass doorstop, which issued forth a loud
brooong. The noise crashed around the room like a long,
wet bullet shredding through porcelain.

My brother bit back a smirk and I tried to stifle a snort
but solemnity ignored our pleas—we erupted, laughter
quaking out our faces into our bodies and through the
floor. We were hopeless, laughing at our laughing, our glee
an infinite rope fraying off in every direction.

It's not that we forgot God or the martyrs or the Prophet's
holy word—quite the opposite, in fact, we were boys built
to love what was in front of our faces: my brother and I on
the floor draped across each other, laughing tears into our
prayer rugs.[3]

Poetry offers forms of belonging that transcend language, culture, and circumstance. As Ashley M. Jones found her voice through Harriet Tubman's story and Kaveh Akbar discovered "amongness" in poetic conversations across millennia, we too can find our place in poetry's embrace. Whether through close readings of a single poem, writing our own verses, or simply memorizing and carrying beloved lines in our hearts, poetry creates space for all parts of our experience—the sacred and profane, the certain and mysterious. Belonging through poetry doesn't require us to be poets ourselves; it asks only that we remain open to how poems might help us feel more fully human, more deeply connected to ourselves and others, more at home in the world.

When you begin to view writing through a lens of belonging, your practice expands to include more than just sitting down and wanting to write. Not that you *need* more than sitting down and wanting to write, but if you have access to extra goodness in the writing life and beyond, why not consider it, seek it, reach for it?

Read a poem. Then, practice noticing what writing is like in light of poetic belonging and give your attention to what appears on the page and throughout your days.

Become

A little clarity, a bit of daring,
some luck, and a great deal of
self-regard. Then life is bountiful.

—Toni Morrison

Writers are always in the process of becoming. To become is to enter the sacred space of transformation, where, through the act of writing, who we are meets who we're not yet. Becoming requires both surrender and trust in the process of change. Each word we write, each revision we make, each story we tell shapes not just the work but the writer.

We are always being formed to write the words we will write tomorrow, next month, next year. The person who begins an essay is not quite the same person who finishes it.

In spiritual direction, we learn to honor the space between being and becoming. This liminal space holds both what is and what might be—the current draft and its potential, the writer we are and the writer we're called to be. Time plays its part here, allowing transformation to unfold at its own pace, like the hours required for bread to rise or the months and years necessary for grief to heal.

Becoming happens in cycles and spirals. As we ride the cycles and travel along the spirals, we return to familiar themes with new understanding, approach old stories from fresh perspectives, revisit early works with deeper wisdom. Each turn of the spiral brings us closer to our authentic voice, our true work, our essential self.

To come to, to arrive, to approach: "become" suggests movement toward something, with a focus on the process rather than the destination. We become through practice, through showing up to the page day after day. We become through community, through sharing our work and receiving feedback. We become through attending to what calls us, what moves us, what won't let us go. To become is to trust that each word written and every story shared moves us closer to who we're meant to be, as writers and as whole human beings.

Become Friends with Time

Twenty years ago, while I was reading Kathleen Norris's book *The Cloister Walk*, Saint Benedict of Nursia became a spiritual guide who transformed my views of time, work, and prayer. Norris introduced me to Benedictine monasticism when I was dabbling in writing, growing my reading practice, and distancing myself from American evangelicalism. Fixed hours of prayer, regular engagement with the psalms, and heightened awareness of the presence of God in all things gave me ways to hold on to my faith as I let go of more and more evangelical tenets that weren't in alignment with Scripture and the love of Jesus. After receiving the good things offered in *The Rule of Saint Benedict* (and ignoring the not-so-good), I continued to grow in my understanding of Benedictine spirituality through personal prayer practices and visits to a Benedictine monastery near my home.

The most transformative gift I've received from Benedictine spirituality was worked out in how I view and inhabit time. Norris describes how attending daily liturgical prayers at St. John's Abbey in Collegeville, Minnesota, for several months helped her grasp why Benedictines refer to their Liturgy of the Hours (also called the Divine Office) as "the sanctification of time."[1] In Saint Benedict's day, the monastic schedule included eight times for communal prayer, although many Benedictine monasteries today have reduced their prayer times to four. For Saint Benedict, prayer was the most important work. Orienting one's schedule around the Divine Office emphasizes lauds and vespers over whatever meaning eight in the morning or the end of a workday might hold. Arranging the day around those sacred moments was a way to embody that conviction.[2]

During the fall of 2023, I returned to the idea of time when my life, writing, and work felt especially scattered and disconnected. I was hoping for a greater sense of cohesion and wanted to create a narrative that would integrate my varied ideas, numerous interests, and related business endeavors. After turning this dilemma over and inspecting it from different perspectives, I received what I was waiting for: What if I let time be a container that holds everything together?

I can't cajole my interests and explorations into one book, onto one website, or within one Instagram account, but time is vast enough, particular enough, and mysterious enough to hold my interests together. Time extends infinitely in both directions, capable of gathering to itself all human experience and endeavor. Time manifests in specific, measurable moments while also being deeply personal in how we experience it.[3] And our perception of time varies dramatically based on circumstances, memory, and emotional state.[4]

While Norris and Saint Benedict were my first guides, increasingly I notice poets and novelists trying to make sense of time. Octavia Butler's *Kindred* explores time through the story of a Black woman transported from

1976 Los Angeles to early nineteenth-century Maryland, forcing her to confront history in a deeply personal way.[5] Marcel Proust's *In Search of Lost Time* demonstrates how memories can stretch and compress time, making the past feel vividly present.[6] Virginia Woolf's *Mrs. Dalloway* examines how a single day can contain an entire life's worth of memories and experiences, showing time's fluidity.[7]

And I see politicians and news pundits trying to make sense of—or just use—time. Candidates for office and elected officials use time-related spin tactics to control narratives, including "pivoting" away from uncomfortable moments and pretending certain things that definitely happened in the past are figments of their constituents' imaginations. News pundits debate the pace of social change and progress.

And just about every spiritual direction conversation with writers is a conversation about some aspect of time. Last week one writer was considering how much time it would take to recover physically, feel more settled, and establish meaningful friendships after a recent move and job change. Another writer has been waiting on responses from publishers about her book manuscript and wants to be better at waiting but can't seem to crack that code. A writer who is a new father keeps experimenting with his writing and prayer schedule with a baby. What used to work no longer works, and he has yet to discover a new system for contemplative practices and creativity that fit well with his new paternal obligations. What could it look like for him to practice belonging to time? How could he repair his relationship with time and work with its natural cycles instead of fighting against them?

While sitting at my kitchen table thinking about these questions, the poem "Perhaps the World Ends Here" by Joy Harjo[8] came to mind. In the poem, Harjo centers the kitchen table as a metaphor for a transformative space where life's cycles unfold—children become adults, raw ingredients transform into nourishing meals, grief spirals into healing, and individual experiences cycle into shared stories through the rituals that occur around this gathering place.

As I contemplated the intersection of this poem, the kitchen table, and time, I began to envision a spiritual practice that would honor time's spiral nature. What if I sat at my kitchen table at one o'clock every afternoon (okay, most afternoons) to witness my relationship with time? Like seasons returning with deeper meaning, this daily practice would allow my kitchen table to welcome all of me—all of my work and confusion, ideas and frustrations, hopes and disappointments, dreams and failures. Each return to the table would build upon previous understanding, like a spiral staircase ascending to new perspectives.

"The world begins at a kitchen table," writes Harjo. "No matter what, we must eat to live." Stacey Balkun reads Harjo's poem with attention to this cyclical spirit. She reflects on how the kitchen table is a domestic space, traditionally considered a woman's space, but it is also a place where life's rhythms manifest. Where minds meet to argue and further ideas, where mothers prepare meals in endless cycles of nourishment, where countless poets shove aside dirty dishes to capture not just events but the underlying patterns of existence.[9]

Perhaps the table—as represented in Harjo's poem, and my actual kitchen table—could be a concrete representation of time's spiral nature. The next day I showed up to my kitchen table at one o'clock. I returned day after day, each session building upon previous insights. Through experimentation and a willingness to play with time's cycles, I tried to grow my sense of wonder and connection. When limitations appeared, I imagined expansions. I asked God to poke holes in my perspective—to grow the possibilities of what time can be.

A breakthrough occurred during one of my one o'clock dates with time when I realized we don't need to be disgruntled whenever time seems to flow against our writing goals and desires. Like a garden path that shifts with the seasons and requires occasional raking or pruning, our calendars can be viewed as flexible templates rather than as rigid structures. Each disruption offers an opportunity to realign with time—even if it requires a bit of erasing and filling in again—allowing our creative practice to become livelier each time we begin anew.

As you examine your relationship with time, consider how interruptions and disruptions are natural parts of life's rhythms, like weather patterns that alter our plans. Instead of fighting these cycles, we can work with them. Befriend time with more interesting narratives that honor both your writing aspirations and unavoidable forces beyond your control. When you are sure you have run out of time, or when interruptions arise, try viewing these moments as necessary parts of your spiral growth rather than as obstacles. Try opening yourself to possibilities instead of being disgruntled and losing hope.

On the Feast of Saint Benedict, I sit down at my kitchen table at one o'clock. I have a copy of Saint Benedict's *The Rule* and my worn paperback of Norris's *The Cloister Walk*. I do a slow reading of the portions underlined and highlighted by past versions of myself that time holds together alongside the entirety of my work and writing and the rest of life. I linger over Norris's wisdom on the artist's vocation: "Art is a lonely calling, and yet paradoxically communal. If artists invent themselves, it is in the service of others. The work of my life is given to others; in fact, the reader completes it."[10] And I heed Saint Benedict's simple reminder toward the end of a chapter filled with teaching on the tools needed for good works: "And finally," he writes, "never lose hope in God's mercy."[11]

I give thanks to God for this work that was begun in me so many years ago through the prayers, psalms, and poems that I return to again and again. I express gratitude for the practices that have brought me to this point in and with time—as a friend instead of a foe. I breathe.

Become Someone Who Writes What Only You Can Write

Here are two questions I hear again and again from writers: Why would anyone want to read what I want to write? Does my writing even matter? My answer: write what only you can write. Explore your own unique stories and what your perspective might offer to ongoing conversations that no one else can offer. Likely you often want to give time and energy to a topic that many people have already addressed—much of literature grapples with the same human quests to find love or heal from betrayal or navigate death. But consider how your perspective and ideas can invite readers into a fresh encounter with the topics that you find compelling. If your mind keeps returning to the theology of grace—or how to grieve—or if you want to write a novel that examines the intersection of grace and grief, ignore the voice ringing from within your soul that says there are plenty of essays, stories, poems, and books about those topics. With sound confidence because you have much to offer, go deeper instead of turning away.

One exercise for going deeper is to make a personal timeline that plots your theme across the different stages of your life. Don't edit yourself. Scribble it all down. Over the course of days, weeks, or even months, add details about memories, scenes, and events that come to mind. What experiences contribute to your unique encounter with grief or grace? Your mom's crisis of faith when you were seven. The nine different moves to nine different states before your high school graduation. The uncle who was a monk and left the monastery at age thirty-seven.

The purpose of this exercise is not necessarily to push you to write about your mom, moving, or monasticism. You're surveying the landscape of your own experiences and interests. How is your curiosity provoked? Which angles most arrest? What about the patterns and themes appearing and reappearing like the pair of cardinals that arrive every morning at the bird feeder by your kitchen window while you're eating eggs and toast?

If you take the time to dig a little deeper, you may decide you don't have anything new to offer. During the second year of my master of fine arts program, I wrote an essay about recovering from an eating disorder, and my instructor responded: "I've read similar essays a dozen times. I'm sure it was good for you to process this, but you should throw it out unless you have something new to add to the conversation." I had put a significant amount of time and energy into the essay, and her response felt deflating at best, offensive at worst. After riding the enormous wave of embarrassment and landing again on dry ground, I had to admit my instructor was right. I had written an essay I had also read a dozen times.

After a few days of considering what I could add to those essays I'd already read, nothing I came up with sounded interesting enough to pursue. I chose to let my essay be what it was—a way to process my eating disorder recovery—and moved on to develop another work-in-progress.

Hear me clearly: You can write about topics others have already written about. But please consider adding fresh angles that may take you further into what you have to offer to ongoing conversations, then see how things unfold. And, since all of life is the writing life, the time and creative effort exerted on anything that ends up in the drawer of scraps are never a waste. Deleted pages and shelved manuscripts have a hand in forming us to do the writing we'll do that has a better future.

Become Familiar with Openings and Closings

Some contemplative Christians refer to the Ignatian movements of consolation and desolation to describe the lifts and dips common to all who live a life of faith. Saint Ignatius's discussion of consolation reads in part, "I call consolation every increase of hope, faith, and charity, and all interior joy that calls and attracts to heavenly things and to the salvation of one's soul, quieting it and giving it peace in its Creator and Lord." And here's some of what he wrote about desolation in his fourth rule: "I call desolation all the contrary of the third rule, such as darkness of soul, disturbance in it, movement to low and earthly things, disquiet from various agitations and temptations, moving to lack of confidence, without hope, without love, finding oneself totally slothful, tepid, sad, and, as if separated from one's Creator and Lord."[1]

Individual experiences of consolation and desolation have their own hues and shadows, but, generally, feeling connected to the divine with a clear awareness of God's goodness and presence marks spiritual consolation. A feeling of disconnection from the divine with a sort of emptiness of soul that makes you wonder why God seems absent marks spiritual desolation. If you apply Ignatius's framework to creativity, creative consolation may include an enhanced alertness to your writerly identity with loads of noticeable positive momentum in your writing practice while creative desolation might occur when words feel too distant, when you question if any of your creative efforts matter, when you are tempted to quit writing altogether.

One pattern that has presented itself in every single writer I've directed is: Whenever there's an opening (or consolation) in the creative realm, there's an opening in the spiritual realm. Whenever there's a closing (or desolation) in one area, there's a closing in the other. Since one soul holds all, it's impossible to navigate the spiritual without affecting the creative, and vice versa.

Here's one story of how the openings and closings of spirituality and creativity run parallel: A few years ago, during an online cowriting session, after all the participants gathered in silence, I asked everyone present to share what they planned to work on during the writing portion of our time together. Since it was Noelani's first time with the group, I invited her to begin with an introduction and provide a few additional details—where she lives (Los Angeles), what she typically likes to write (screenplays, essays, and poems), how she found her way to the group (online ad). Then, when it was time for her to share what she wanted to work on during the writing time, she paused, took a deep breath that might've been more like a sigh, and said, "I just want to get some words on the page. Maybe begin writing a poem. I haven't written anything in years." I thanked her for joining us and wished her good things for her first cowriting session. She ended up starting a new poem and seemed pleased to have participated.

A few days later, Noelani and I had a one-on-one call, and I asked why she hadn't written in the last few years. She didn't have a clear answer but chalked it up to the demands of parenting three kids, caring for aging parents, two enormous losses, grief. Then I asked the question I usually ask after someone tells me they aren't writing: "How's your spiritual life?"

"Not great. I don't feel much of anything. I don't pray. I feel disconnected from God."

"When did you begin feeling that way? Was it around the time you stopped writing?"

Then silence. Tears. An epiphany.

Here's what Noelani discovered: No opening lasts forever and no closing is final, so having a long view of consolations and desolations as part of a larger spiraling movement will provide a more accurate representation of the spiritual and creative life. Becoming curious about the interactions between the spiritual and creative realms and their movements over time increases your ability to notice the openings and closings in both areas and use them to your advantage, even when you aren't entirely sure what's happening with your faith or your writing practice. If there's a constriction in one area, examine the other area. Do you recognize a similar constriction or sense of being stuck?

If you haven't written in a long time, or if you feel zero energy around writing, take some time to consider what's been going on with you from a spiritual standpoint. Has something happened that made you shut down spiritually? If you're experiencing a season of enormous spiritual growth, how is your writing practice growing too? Once I started seeing this correlation in the writers with whom I worked, I began noticing similar patterns and cycles in my own life: When I am writing, I tend to pray more, and more freely. And if I feel distant from God, I can write my way toward greater spiritual intimacy. Even if it's only a single sentence or paragraph, whenever I write, I find some spiritual opening. When a couple of weeks (or more!) pass without any writing time, I can pray a psalm, pray a round of *visio divina*, or engage with another contemplative practice—and then return to my typical writing practice, or at least inch a bit closer through a few minutes of note taking.

Our writing and faith are intertwined. If you feel shut down creatively, don't worry so much about the cause. See if you can find a doorway to more spiritual depth through breath prayer, a walk in a labyrinth, the singing of a hymn. Then see what that spiritual practice does to your creative practice. If you feel spiritually numb, give more time and attention to your creative expression through a generative prompt or revision exercise. Then notice what happens with your soul.

You may begin to discern regular peaks and lulls with your creative and spiritual energies. Maybe certain seasons of the year or times of the month tend to be more expansive or more restricted. Or you've realized Sunday nights are good for watching your favorite TV show instead of trying to add another five stanzas to that poem in progress. What's closed may not let you in for longer than you prefer. But things that are closed have the potential to open back up. Doors, envelopes, hearts; paragraphs, poems.

Become More at Peace with Uncertainty

When will I have more time to write? When will I have energy to write? What if no one ever reads my work? What if I don't get an agent? What if I never get a book deal? How exactly am I supposed to build a platform and do the writing I need to do?

When these questions and the uncertainty beneath them monopolize your mind, it's hard to develop a joyful, fulfilling creative practice. Instead of being paralyzed by all the "what ifs" and "oh nos," try addressing your uncertainty with narratives that help you imagine many possible outcomes. John Kay and Mervyn King, authors of *Radical Uncertainty: Decision-Making Beyond the Numbers*, suggest acknowledging that no one knows what the future holds. Then make plans for various possibilities and practice resilience for when things don't go the way you prefer.[1]

Visualization can be a helpful tool for this imaginative work. Picture your writing life unfolding as you wish it will unfold—much spacious and sun-drenched writing time, a book of sonnets praised by Marie Howe, whatever it is you most desire. Let the scene come to life in your mind. Embellish it with sensory details. What images can you see while reading one of your poems in your dream publication? What aromas fill the room? How does it feel to hold the magazine in your hands?

Then, similarly visualize receiving a rejection from your dream publication. Practice this negative experience. What physical sensations do you feel in your body when you receive the rejection? Where are you sitting or standing? What sounds do you hear?

Then imagine a few additional outcomes. What else might happen? What are other realistic possibilities?

If you are a person of faith, consider how your religious beliefs and theology intersect with your uncertainty. How can you sink into your beliefs about the divine, and who you are in light of the divine? If you experience assurance of God's involvement in every aspect of your life, how can you lean into your faith to dampen the negative effects of uncertainty?

Uncertainty isn't always bad, especially in the writing process. In an essay about how artificial intelligence is affecting creative-writing students, Meghan O'Rourke closed with astute thoughts on one benefit of uncertainty: "When I write, the process is full of risk, error and painstaking self-correction. It arrives somewhere surprising only when I've stayed in uncertainty long enough to find out what I had initially failed to understand. This attention to the world is worth trying to preserve: The act of care that makes meaning—or insight—possible. To do so will require thought and work."[2]

Uncertainty can invite us to linger in the unknowing and wait for a surprising revelation. It can also move us toward others to seek solutions, comfort, and understanding in community. "Humans thrive in conditions of radical uncertainty when creative individuals can draw on collective intelligence" and "hone their ideas in communication with others," according to Kay and King.[3] So, here are two more questions to consider: How can your uncertainty help you pause and allow enough time for surprise? How can your uncertainty help you belong to other people? Perhaps it would help to reach out to a few trusted confidants and hear their thoughts on your various dilemmas. Let the people who care about you divide your sorrows, slice your worries, and dice your anxieties into more digestible pieces.

Become Comfortable Asking More Questions

When the *Sites of Memory* exhibit at Princeton's Firestone Library honoring Toni Morrison and her writing opened at ten o'clock, I was the first person to enter. I placed my bag on the floor near the security guard and stayed for two and a half hours, wandering among evidence of Morrison's creative process. As I took in the hand-drawn diagrams and maps that accompanied her fiction drafts, I jotted down my own notes and recorded voice memos (photos, alas, weren't allowed, but I think writing notes rather than relying on my camera in fact connected me more deeply to the material).

The exhibit invited me to encounter history, and to be impressed, again, by the power of Morrison's storytelling. Each artifact, photograph, and excerpt spoke of Morrison's indelible mark on American literature and testified to her loyalty to the craft of writing.

After making my way through all the archival materials, I sat on an upholstered bench at the back of the gallery and watched yet another interview. Morrison was talking to psychologist Sigmund Koch and literary critic Hortense Spillers in footage culled from eight hours of conversations. At one point, Koch asked Morrison about her creative process and how her novel *Beloved* came to be.

After Morrison described the origin of *Beloved*—the story was seeded by an 1855 newspaper account of a woman who killed one of her daughters to prevent her re-enslavement—she said this: "I was concentrating on just the act. And I thought, 'She did this noble, horrible thing, perfectly necessary and perfectly awful. . . . Suppose that little girl had any say so, any say so in the matter. Suppose she thought it wasn't a high idea and had the opportunity to say so, what would the mother say? What would happen to [the mother's] rationale if [the daughter] had an opportunity to say, 'What did you do that for?'" That was one of the inroads.

Later, Morrison offered additional questions she used in the early stages of writing new fiction. There's "a sort of stewing period that precedes the writing" where she considered things like, "What must it have been like? What then would it be like for the other? What would that have done to that person? What would she have meant by . . . ? What would she have felt by . . . ? Et cetera."

Morrison's description of her writing process helped me better comprehend the role questions play in the openings and closings between the creative and spiritual spheres. Asking questions can invite that which is in the shadows to come into the light. Questions pry open spaces where certainty had been suffocating imagination, giving oxygen to the unsaid and the unsayable. When Morrison asked, "What would the mother say?" or "What would that have done to that person?" she wasn't seeking specific answers—she was creating conditions for the complexity of human experience to breathe. This is the alchemy of questioning: It turns flat narratives into living worlds. By leaning into the "what ifs" and "why nots," we learn to dwell in the fertile gaps between knowing and unknowing, where authentic stories are nurtured. Questions teach us to write with mystery rather than against it, trusting that the act of asking is a form of revelation.

"Speculative Futures," the final section of the Morrison exhibit, prompted me to think about the purpose of archives. This section displayed pieces of projects that were never finished or published, fragments that "bear witness to Toni Morrison's always capacious imagination, to her commitment to creative risk taking and experimentation."[1] Placards prompted visitors to rethink archives not as repositories of answers but as sites that generate questions: What if we read archives for possibilities rather than for facts? What if their mood is the subjunctive—the mood of "what could be"?

These ideas echoed Morrison's Nobel lecture, where she declared storytelling an act of radical creation: "Narrative is radical, creating us at the very moment it is being created. . . . Language alone protects us from the scariness of things with no names. Language alone is meditation." Her words remind us that writing is not about perfection but about continuing to show up and keep trying. To write is to ask, "What has the world been to you in the dark places and in the light?"—and to trust that the act of asking clears a path through the unknown.[2]

Leaving the exhibit, I carried this truth: Writing, like faith, thrives in the unfinished. Sometimes we may lose hold of the full and perfect story, but we can engage with fragments—light and shadow, joy and despair—by questioning with curiosity instead of fear. Morrison's legacy teaches us that survival, creativity, and spirituality are not linear journeys but ongoing dialogues. When we ask questions, we align with the subjunctive mood of existence, where every "what if" dissolves the thick fog of fear and allows fresh hopes and probabilities to appear along the continuous, winding path.

Become Even More Curious

Curiosity has long driven human discovery and creative expression, often transcending social boundaries in unexpected ways. In the eighteenth century, as Susan Scott Parrish documents, there was so much curiosity about the flora and fauna of the so-called New World that women in the British colonies were invited into the work of scientific discourse, of stargazing and botanical-specimen collecting, in ways they would not have been in Europe:

> Colonial women roamed "in the Wilds" digging up flowering plants, squelched along the shore in search of bivalves, drew outlines of hundreds of leaves, carefully packed butterflies to reach catalogers in Europe, filled silk bags with quantities of seeds, or rose early to measure comets because, as Eliza Lucas Pinckney put it, they "love[d] the vegitable [or animal or celestial] world extremely." Moreover, these women understood the unique historical and geographical place they occupied. Living in a world of which the ancients knew nothing, they saw shells, quadrupeds, birds, and butterflies that the Old World had an inexhaustible curiosity to behold.

Elite women did some of that roaming and digging themselves, but many also tasked their servants, free and enslaved, to do the manual work entailed in discovery.[1]

What's particularly striking about this historical example is how curiosity opened doors for women to engage in activities and traverse landscapes that local gender norms would otherwise have prohibited. Curiosity carries us into places we would not otherwise go.

And curiosity lies underneath all lively literature—literature produced in the grip of inquiry, rather than writing that simply rehearses what the writer already knew before she sat down at her desk. In his book *Curious: The Desire to Know and Why Your Future Depends on It*, Ian Leslie writes, "If you allow yourself to become incurious, your life will be drained of color, interest, and pleasure. You will be less likely to achieve your potential at work or in your creative life. While barely noticing it, you'll become a little duller, a little dimmer." He says this dulling and dimming can happen to any of us. Curiosity keeps the clouds away, protects the brightness.[2] Without curiosity we become grayscale rainy versions of ourselves.

Curiosity fuels our writing, freshens our thoughts on timeless topics, and opens our eyes to see new ways of doing things. The curiosity muscles that expand and deflate when we sit down to write can also pump and relax as we explore our relationship to creative work, make discoveries about our individual process and goals, and reveal unpredictable solutions to the familiar obstacles that keep us from having the writing life we want.

Writers who honor their curiosity are willing to admit there's always so much they don't know while facing the possibility that what they do know might no longer be true.

They care less about what others think. They have fewer obstacles to authenticity. They seek creative solutions to the resistance that keeps them from their writing practice. And they become more concerned with their own writing process preferences than with how others make their art.

Curiosity moves us closer to creative freedom by removing excessive and unnecessary expectations. When I sit down to write with no curiosity—when I think I already know exactly what I want to say—I, at best, miss the joy of process in pursuit of a finished product (and usually the finished product is not very good—not original, not surprising). When I bring curiosity to the page, I am honoring my underlying desire to let my mind wander toward new discoveries and remaining open to whatever good things I might bump into along the way.

Recently, a writer friend asked what I do when I get bored. Without any hesitation, I answered, "I don't get bored." That's probably not true, but I honestly don't remember being bored because often, when I feel a tinge of boredom, I become curious about why I might be getting bored. The curiosity immediately outruns the boredom.

John Cage once wrote, "In Zen they say: If something is boring after two minutes, try it for four. If still boring, try it for eight, sixteen, thirty-two, and so on. Eventually one discovers that it's not boring at all but very interesting."[3] Practicing attention and moving toward something that appears boring at first may be the escape route from the dulling or dimming. The extraordinary is revealed within the mundane, establishing additional pathways for creative expression and reconnecting us to the sense of wonder and curiosity that drew us to writing in the first place.

Become a Writer Who Follows the Energy

When directees are in the middle of drafting a new project, they often want to discuss their work-in-progress.

One directee set up a session to determine why he was stuck drafting chapter 7 of his new book. At the beginning of our hour together, I asked him to give me an overview of his writing process *before* he felt stuck, and any thoughts on what might be causing the shift he'd experienced. After a fifteen-minute explanation of how beautifully his writing practice had unfolded during the previous six months for the first six chapters of his book, he described how it had become impossible to work on chapter 7. He was allocating one month to complete the first draft of each chapter and hadn't made any progress for the past two weeks. He was halfway through the month with no new words and was concerned about getting further behind and losing control of the entire project.

Next, I asked him to share the list of the remaining chapter titles for the rest of the book. He opened the document and read the table of contents for chapters 8 through 12. Then I posed this question: "Which unwritten chapter on that list feels more connected to your present life experiences? Which topic has more energy right now?"

"Chapter 9. No doubt."

"Can you put chapter 7 aside for now and skip ahead to chapter 9? Instead of writing the chapters in order, can you follow the energy?"

His eyes lit up at the suggestion and he began laughing. "I can't believe I didn't think of this myself."

It's so easy to let a predetermined plan dictate the path to completing a task or accomplishing a goal. If you assess the energy you have for different pieces of the whole and allow them to be guiding lights, you might find your way through to the other side with less resistance.

Notice:

- which part of the project is most aligned with the reality of your present moment.
- which part of the project is most aligned with your most active curiosities.
- which part of the project triggers resistance within you.

Other questions to consider: How do your body, mind, and soul respond to the flow of creative energy? How do you decide how to follow it? What plans might you reconsider today?

Become Someone Who Arrives Early and Stays Late

I'm sitting by the entrance to the DMV satellite office on Highway 31 in my camping chair that I've never used for camping, and I'm first in line. It's six forty in the morning and the birds are loud. So many birds are hollering here in this retail strip in the burbs with a grocery store and a Starbucks just beyond the parking lot. Why are there so many birds with only a few crepe myrtles here and there? I notice my first crepe myrtle blooms of the season. White. Over by the Publix.

When I arrived and saw all the empty parking spaces, I wondered if it was unnecessary, getting here so early. But while I gather my belongings, another woman drives up. As I am settling into my spot by the door, she lifts a small wooden collapsible stool out of the back of her SUV, leans it against the side of the building to save her place behind me, then returns to the comfort of her Tahoe. I wonder if she ever uses her stool for camping.

A man arrives five or so minutes later. Now we have a proper line going. He's pacing while smoking a cigarette and talking on his phone. He's telling whoever's on the other end that their health needs to come first. He's repeating it again and again, as if speaking it will create a new reality. "Your health comes first. That should guide every choice you make. Your health comes first." Cigarette smoke swirls around me, and now I need another shower.

I've been sitting here for thirty minutes. Huge, insulated mug. Headphones. Laptop. I've been writing and reading about grief. I start crying, while remembering my dad and the grief I experienced after he died. I cry behind my sunglasses while others join the line.

A cheerful woman in a pink twinset walks past me to claim her spot. "You're smart for bringing a chair!" she chirps. I've been participating in Jami Attenberg's 1000 Words of Summer, and I'm using this writing challenge to finish up my book proposal. I don't usually write every day, but, during Attenberg's first challenge several years ago, I discovered that writing one thousand words every day for fourteen days is realistic for me, so I've repeated Attenberg's challenge several times. I smile at the woman in the twinset and think: *The smart thing is getting my thousand words in before my busy day*. Nothing will be hanging over my head as I check items off my list. Renew license. Deposit a check. Return library books. Drive to North Carolina. Host a conference call.

My fourteen-thousand-plus words that come together during every 1000 Words of Summer challenge are never stellar. But they are words I can use and revise. It takes more effort and time to write one thousand words in a day than it used to. Remember how we all thought we had early-onset dementia during the COVID-19 pandemic? Our minds and bodies have been through so much over the last several years. Sometimes I still can't remember the words I need. Sitting there in front of the DMV, I think about how my chronic pain is larger. About how I want to figure out better ways to exist as a writer in this world full of so much pain and grief and forgetfulness.

Bereavement. That's the word I was looking for.

The DMV will open in ten minutes. The woman climbs out of her Tahoe to take her place in line behind me. No one appears bothered by the fact that she just waited in her car for forty-five minutes and is now claiming her spot.

Right before the DMV opens, I save my place in line by placing the oversized mug on the ground where I've been sitting and return my chair and other belongings to the trunk of my car. It only takes ten minutes to renew my license. Before driving to the bank, I grab my computer and write in my car for another fifteen minutes to get my thousand words for the day. I roll the windows down because it's not too hot yet. I write while the birds sing and the line outside the DMV extends down the entire length of the building's sidewalk. I exceed my goal.

Become Comfortable Writing Everywhere

Here's a list of some of the places I've written. What is your list? And what's your list of places where you'd like to write in the future?

At my desk and the kitchen table
In my bathroom writing nooks
On the sofa and while lying in bed
On porches and in yards surrounded by books
At the park on a bench and once in a hammock
At a rest stop off Interstate 59 heading south
In parking lots, carpool lines, and driveways
Coffee shops and restaurants, sitting at the bar
In bookstores, libraries, and food courts at the mall
Coworking spots all over this city
Hotel rooms, hotel lobbies, hotel patios
Museum galleries and museum cafés
Early mornings on the beach
While walking down plenty of streets
In a dozen airports and as many planes
On a ferry and on a train
During too many AAU basketball tournaments
On the bleachers at my godson's T-ball practice
In Asheville, Durham, Raleigh, and Winston-Salem

Knoxville, Nashville, Memphis, Chattanooga
Panama City, Seagrove, Seaside, and Destin
New Jersey, New York, Pennsylvania, Massachusetts
New Mexico, Washington, South Carolina, and Georgia
West Virginia, Connecticut, Mississippi, Louisiana

Some here, some there, pretty much everywhere.

Become a Writer Who Pauses

When we notice we're living as if everything depends on us—work, creative endeavors, relationships, movement toward health and wholeness—it's time to pause.

And breathe.

Linger in the stillness.

And be.

Pauses are helpful during more mundane times too. Maybe you need to undo the effects of what has felt like too much time scrolling on social media. Maybe you're sad. Maybe you're bored. Maybe you're lonely. Maybe things are rocking along pretty well; you're fine. Fine is good. Maybe you're happy and you want to savor the moment.

I've never met anyone who regretted pausing. Taking a few breaths or a few minutes to slow down and connect to the present moment creates a more attentive inhabiting of subsequent moments. Some people pause at the top of every hour to give soulful attention to their bodies and minds while checking in with their current perception of time. Others are more willy-nilly and let their gut lead their pauses with no agenda, no checklist of to-do items

Another way I love to pause is to stop doing whatever I'm doing and read a poem. Sometimes I read a poem in the context of a larger ritual. Sometimes I simply walk over to the bookshelf in my living room that holds most of my books of poetry, select a volume, open it, and read whichever poem appears on the page before me. Other times I open the Google doc containing a list of favorite poems that I've gathered like stones of remembrance. This list of soul poems serves as a prayer book of sorts. Many of these poems have accompanied me through years of ordinary and extraordinary moments. Some are new, read only once, waiting to join me for a walk down a future path toward something I can't yet imagine. When I pause with a favorite poem that contains memories and points of connection to past times and former versions of myself, I still try to let the text meet me in that exact moment.

I can't remember the first time I read "Transformation" by Adam Zagajewski, but I remember how it spoke to my soul because it does still. I love how the poem begins with a confession. The narrator hasn't been writing. It's been months since he last wrote a single poem. Even though I know what's coming, the first two lines prompt my curiosity. The poem asks why I haven't been writing. Perhaps this question is for you, too. Have you been writing? If not, why?

The speaker responds with a list of things he's done instead: reading the paper, thinking about power structures, watching sunsets, listening to birds, taking walks. And at the end, he pulls back the veil on the one thing he wants: "lightning/transformation/you."[1] Zagajewski might have used a single word for the one thing the poem's narrator wants, but he chose three. So, every time I read this poem I think about how lightning, transformation, and "you" can satisfy a sole craving. A specific object of love, lust, or desire. Rest, maybe? God? "Tell me more," I say to the poem's speaker. What do you want? What is the object at hand that requires three different words when one might suffice? Then I ask myself the same question. What do I want?

"Transformation" also exemplifies how all of life is the writing life. While the poem's narrator hasn't written a poem in months, he has lived. He has encountered beauty and tension. With much care and thoughtfulness, and perhaps plenty of pauses, he has recognized his longing and formed a trinity of want. All the living he's done has helped him become the person who will eventually sit down and write "Transformation."

Pausing with this poem transforms me. I arrive anxious and leave with more peace. I arrive with doubt and leave with more belief. I arrive holding my breath and leave with slow, deep inhales and exhales.

Become a Writer Who Sits Alone in Silence

According to a report that analyzed eleven different research studies, 67 percent of people would rather stick their finger in an electric socket than sit in silence alone with their thoughts.[1] Maybe writing can be hard at times because sitting alone in silence is hard.

While there are ways to make the writing life less isolating, the activity required—putting words on paper, typing words on a screen—is an individual sport, often done in solitude and silence. Even if you prefer to listen to a favorite playlist or sit at a table in a bustling food court, writing requires a kind of inner quiet stillness—and sitting alone in auditory silence from time to time can be helpful for the creative process.

Janet Frame explained the role of silence for writers in her autobiography, *An Angel at My Table*. While living in a small army hut behind Auckland writer Frank Sargeson's home after his generous offer of time and space in which Frame could develop her writing career, Frame discovered how quiet solitude affects her creativity:

> Within the first week of my stay he drew attention to this. "You babble at breakfast," he said. I took note

> of what he said and in future I refrained from "babbling," but it was not until I had been writing regularly each day that I understood the importance to each of us of forming, holding, maintaining our inner world, and how it was renewed each day on waking, how it even remained during sleep, like an animal outside the door waiting to come in; and how its form and power were protected most by surrounding silence. My hurt at being called a "babbler" faded as I learned more of the life of a writer.[2]

Frame and Sargeson talked plenty, too. They discussed writing—their own and others'. They read the same books together and marveled at Proust, Tolstoy, or Faulkner over suppers of paella and wine. And they shared long meals and longer conversations with larger groups of Sargeson's friends and other young writers. But periods of silence were necessary and woven throughout the rhythms of their days.

Both writers had their own practices of solitude, as well, with regular cycles of work, rest, and walks along the streets of Takapuna or on the shore of a nearby beach. Frame found herself anxious and distracted if she could hear Sargeson rustling about in the garden on the other side of her hut's wall and would type things such as "The quick brown fox jumps over the lazy dog" and "Now is the time for all good men to come to the aid of the party" again and again on her Remington until he went back inside his house.[3]

Silence creates space for the mind to calm and the unexpected to emerge. In quiet moments, we can hear whispers of our deeper selves, notice subtle connections between seemingly unrelated ideas, allow our thoughts to wander into unexplored territory, or simply slow our cognitive activity. This kind of deep listening—to ourselves, to the world around us, to what wants to be written—requires periods of genuine solitude. When we step away from the noise of daily life, even briefly, we create room for our creative voice to strengthen and clarify.

Interweaving periods of focused silence and solitude with writing sessions or activities that allow for engagement with other people or interesting ideas is a helpful way to structure a writing day, a solo writing retreat, or an hour-long reset. A cyclical approach that alternates rest and work, conversation and quiet, mimics cycles we see in the natural world and results in more sustained energy for our thoughts and word count over time.

If adding stretches of silence and solitude to your writing life makes you want to stick your finger in a socket, consider taking a gentle step toward cultivating a solitude practice. Focus on your breathing for five minutes. Give all your attention to your inhale and exhale. Listen to each cycle of breath. Feel the air enter your nose and lungs, feel the release. Notice what happens to your body as you do this intentional breathing. What do you let go of? What are you still holding on to?

When we take time to anchor our attention to a single focus like the breath or ground our senses, the body and nervous system slow down, and stress dissipates. Cortisol and adrenaline levels decrease, allowing you to relax more easily. The more you practice sitting in silence, the easier it becomes. Mindful practitioner Elaine Smookler explains the transformations that happen as we become more comfortable with sitting in silence. "You're able to let go, to not feel afraid to be alone. . . . You can begin to enjoy what it's like to be with yourself and feel calm. And as you learn to be alone you can learn how to be brave and honest with how things are right now."[4] When you become better at being alone, you might experience greater levels of contentment and fewer obstacles to creativity.

Become Someone Who Writes in the Dark

Much of life begins in the dark. Butterflies begin in the darkness of cocoons. Birds begin in the darkness of eggs. Plants begin in the darkness of seeds. Experiences of darkness tend to precede experiences of light. "Let there be light" cannot be uttered without a prerequisite darkness.

Night has typically been a fraught time for me. I'm not one who sleeps straight through the night—my sleep is complicated and adventurous. Night is also when I am prone to spiral down into negativity. Prone to think I should quit writing or spiritual direction or the church or all of it. When I start spiraling downward, I go to bed early because I know everything is always better the next morning.

Learning that the Jewish Sabbath is observed from sunset on Friday to sunset on Saturday gave me a new understanding of darkness and night. Viewing the night as the beginning turns my view of time upside down and freshens my perspective of nighttime.

Ismar Schorsch wrote that celebrating Shabbat from sunset to sunset helps one "experience the passage of time each day consciously and bravely." He continues: "When envisioned as the start of a new day, night loses its dread. It becomes a time of preparation, renewal and anticipation, a period of incubation before a new birth."[1]

Right now, the sun is setting, and darkness will soon descend, and reading those words gives me a sense of safety I wasn't searching for. Turning out the lights and going to bed is one way to quit, but it's also one way to begin again. Viewing darkness as a beginning makes it easier to embrace the good things that can come during the hours when one is awake but should be asleep: new ideas for a recipe to try, possible solutions to relationship problems, additional insights into how to rearrange your furniture or your pantry or your spices. The mind and soul can do some of their best work in the quiet darkness. They might capture the perfect verb for that essay in progress. Or figure out a chapter ending that will create a better transition to what's coming next in the novel you're almost finished with. Or dream up a new Instagram post. Creative connections establish more smoothly in the dark. There are fewer obstacles. The body's senses are stilled and its systems are slowed, so there's more room for creativity to move.

Unfortunately, when our creativity has more elbow room, our anxieties do too. Blank space fills with the wrestlings of old deep fears and new shallow doubts when I'm in bed and know I need to sleep but sleep isn't coming easy because that spot on the left side of my neck is bothering me again and I'm facing the full contents of all of those bags my mind has been toting around since the last time I turned out the lights and climbed in bed.

But sometimes those dark hours are full of goodness and gratitude. Sometimes, when the lights are out, I tell

God or myself or the universe "thank you." Thank you for my work and family and friends and this fullness of soul right now in the dark when everything is quiet and all distractions are far away. Sometimes the darkness is full of promise because I've slowed down enough to process my latest curiosities, most recent questions, and those connections I noticed twelve hours earlier and made a mental note to explore later but didn't and now I'm lying here in the dark in my bed and my neck is fine and I have five new ideas, five good ideas for the writing I didn't do during the daylight hours.

When writers say they don't know when or what or how to write the things they want to write—when they are in a place of not knowing—perhaps they are simply in that space one inhabits before the light arrives. When they are in the dark creatively, they are in the darkness of beginnings. The ideas and insights will come. Words are born into morning's light from the womb's midnight.

Sometimes writing begins in the dark in a more obvious manner. I grab my phone from the nightstand and send myself emails because this is what I do. I don't want to turn on a light or write with a pen and paper because I don't want to stir my senses too much. After I send the emails, I ask God to help me remember to open those emails the next day when I take the time to write in the light. And I know the next morning I will prepare my workspace and write for hours and hours because I'm staying at a friend's house in a different state so I can write without my family needing me. I will take breaks for walks in between the writing sessions because walking undoes the harmful effects of all of that sitting and typing. I will read, too, because I know other writers have good ideas about my ideas, and I will pray or think about praying because I know I'm not doing any of this by myself. What began in the dark continues in the light.

If you're interested in receiving what the darkness has to offer, drink a caffeinated beverage later than usual, do some stretches to wake your body up a bit, and have a four-hour solo writing retreat at night. Make sure your schedule the next day will allow for extra sleep and low-energy activities.

You can have your night retreat at home. You can borrow a friend's guest room or go to a local hotel.

As you plan your retreat, you might make a playlist with songs about darkness, or a reading list and online art selections that explore themes of nighttime.

As your retreat begins, sit in a comfortable spot and watch the darkness descend. Settle down about thirty minutes before the official sunset time for this day and location (which can be found online easily) and stay still and silent while the darkness grows over the next hour or so. Take voice memo notes if you like. Or try to be present to the entire experience without taking notes. It might be nice to try it one night without taking notes, then another night while taking notes.

Respond to the following questions and prompts in your journal or in a new essay, story, poem, or letter to a friend:

- What is an early memory of darkness and nighttime? Include as many sensory details as possible.
- What films and TV shows come to mind when you

think of nighttime and darkness? Why? Can you describe the scenes or circumstances?

- What happens in the dark in your city or town, neighborhood, and yard? What stirs? What settles?

Become a Little Neurotic

When Saint Teresa of Avila sent the second draft of *The Book of Her Life* to her spiritual director, she reminded him that he promised to tear up the bad parts. She listed all kinds of reasons why the manuscript was not shiny and sparkly. She begged for feedback and validation. She was a neurotic writer too! Just like the rest of us!

We all have our moments; some writers are just better at hiding it. Writing can wring you out, turn you inside out, make you wonder Why Do We Even Do This? We write because it's a huge part of who we are. And sometimes things get a little dramatic. Here's a portion of the note Saint Teresa of Avila included with the second draft of *The Book of Her Life*:

> I did what your Reverence commanded me and enlarged upon the material. I did this on the condition that you do what you promised by tearing up what appears to you to be bad. I hadn't finished reading it after the writing was done when you sent for it. It could be that some of the things are poorly explained and others put down twice, for I had so little time I couldn't read over what I wrote. I ask you to correct it and have it transcribed if it is to be brought to Padre

> Maestro Avila, for it could happen that someone might recognize my handwriting. I urgently desire that he be asked for his opinion about it, since this was my intention in beginning to write.[1]

If Saint Teresa of Avila can freak out about her writing, we can freak out about our writing—and about everything that comes with the business of writing and the other work that is tangentially connected to our writing.

Familiar writerly neuroses include letting the publishing process interfere with your writing practice, giving social media more power than it deserves, and spending too much energy comparing your writing life to others' paths. When your inner world is on edge, remind yourself that this happens to other writers too—you aren't alone. Then return to the basics. Remember why you write, be more intentional about your nourishing rhythms, perhaps establish a new ritual.

Feeling a little (or a lot) neurotic about your writing or your writing life might be a sign that your brain needs a break from words. Here are suggestions for a contemplative drawing practice to do as a prewriting ritual that might serve as an end run around the neuroses. Do this by hand, with pen or pencil and paper.

- Write down seven objects that you see right now.
- Write down seven colors that you see right now.
- Write down seven words that come to mind while noticing and giving attention to your surroundings.
- Write down three memories that come to mind that are connected to the space you are inhabiting.

- Take a few deep breaths.
- Pick something you see and draw it. This can be an entire section of the room or a single couch cushion. The focus is not on perfecting the drawing; the focus is on noticing your surroundings.
- Write three sentences. Then three more.

Become Through Liturgy

During the last several years of my time in evangelicalism, I occasionally attended morning prayer at an Episcopal church. Now, my husband and I worship regularly with an Episcopal congregation one block over from our house. The Episcopal Church's liturgies, found chiefly in the Book of Common Prayer,[1] make me feel safe and a part of something bigger than myself. I know what to expect and when to expect it. I utter familiar prayers alongside a worldwide communion. Being in the Episcopal Church gives me a greater sense of rest because none of what happens during a service is dependent on me figuring anything out. I enter. I participate alongside others. I receive.

When I began leading cowriting sessions on Zoom in 2021, I incorporated liturgical elements inspired by my growing acquaintance with the Episcopal Church to create a similar sense of safety and familiarity. Participants would know what to expect and when to expect it.

At one Saturday morning session, a regular participant named Patricia joined late, noting in the chat that she wished to remain silent to "navigate a hard morning." After a bit more opening conversation, typed and spoken, the group moved through our familiar, liturgical rhythm: We each stated our intention for our writing time. Then we drew six deep breaths; then an invocation using a poem (on this morning Edna St. Vincent Millay's "What Lips My Lips Have Kissed, and Where, and Why");[2] then thirty minutes of writing time.

When we reconvened, Patricia surprised us by speaking up about the poem. A retired high school English teacher, she had taught it many times as a sad reflection on loss, but that morning she saw something new: "The tree knows the summers that sang in it sing no more, but that's okay. . . . The poem is not as sad as I thought because more summers are coming."

The liturgical elements helped Patricia find a posture of reception that morning, leading to fresh insight despite her difficult start. Her beautiful noticing—that past summers make way for future ones—gave life and light to everyone present.

The relationship between liturgical prayer and writing runs deeper than mere structure. Just as liturgy connects us to centuries of faithful practice without requiring us to generate fresh words each time, writing within established forms—whether sestinas or essays—allows us to step into streams of tradition that carry us forward. Sometimes we may not "feel" particularly inspired during either practice, but showing up faithfully often leads to unexpected moments of grace. The words are already there, waiting for us to embrace and use them.

Like liturgical prayer that joins our voice with countless others across time and distance, writing connects us intimately with both readers and other writers. When we write, we enter a vast conversation that extends beyond our immediate experience. Just as praying the psalms puts us in communion with generations of others who have voiced the same hopes and laments, writing places our individual experience within a larger human story. Regardless of the form our writing takes, we're participating in ancient patterns of meaning-making that transform both writer and reader. And the rhythmic nature of liturgy provides a model for creative practice. As Eugene Peterson notes, "Liturgy keeps us in touch with the story as it defines and shapes our beginnings and ends, our living and dying."[3] Similarly, writing rhythms—through daily practice or seasonal cycles—help structure our creative life and connect us to something larger than ourselves while transcending our immediate circumstances.

The elements of becoming we've explored—from writing what only you can write to embracing liturgy—work together like ingredients in a well-loved soup recipe. You can combine them in various ways or use them individually, depending on what nourishment you need in any given moment. Whether you have ten minutes in the carpool line or a quiet pocket of time between lunch and dinner, these practices can provide structure and sustenance for your creative life.

Follow Patricia's lead of discovering new meaning in a familiar poem and allow each return to these elements to bring you fresh insights. You might start with meditative breathing while waiting to pick up your child or read a favorite poem before beginning your workday. Perhaps you'll create your own mini-liturgy for that precious half hour between meetings. The key isn't perfection or complexity but rather finding ways to weave practices of stillness, creativity, and inspiration into the regular rhythms of your days.

Behold

The object isn't to make art, it's to be in that wonderful state which makes art inevitable.

—Robert Henri

Writers are called to be beholders, keeping watch over the details others might miss. We notice how light falls through winter branches, how grief settles in the shoulders, how joy arrives unexpectedly during a morning run. This attentive presence enriches both our writing and our spiritual selves, helping us find meaning in the entire scope of our daily lives.

To behold is to witness with your whole being—not just seeing but receiving, not just observing but opening to what's being given. Like Mary Oliver stopping to marvel at a grasshopper's mechanics or Gerard Manley Hopkins discovering the "inscape" of ordinary things,[1] *beholding transforms both the observer and the observed.*

To keep, to watch over, to have in sight: "behold" suggests a responsibility, a sacred task of attention. When we truly behold something—a wisteria vine, a child's gesture, a moment of grace—we develop a relationship with it. We move beyond mere observation into contemplation, beyond surface seeing into deeper layers of knowing.

In spiritual direction, we practice beholding together. We notice the divine showing up in unexpected places—in creative resistance and breakthroughs, in daily rituals and dramatic transformations, in the spaces between words and the silence that holds them. This kind of seeing changes us and prepares us to receive what each moment offers.

Beholding requires slowing down, creating space, cultivating presence. We trade productivity for receptivity, rushing for rest, doing for being, knowing for mystery. When we truly notice—whether through writing, prayer, or simple presence—ordinary moments reveal their extraordinary depths, and everyday experiences become doorways to greater understanding.

To behold is to remember that we write not just with our minds but with our whole selves—body, spirit, memory, imagination—all working together to translate what we witness into words that might transform us and help others see anew.

Behold Through Contemplation

Contemplatives maintain a strong awareness of the present moment. They prefer slower, quieter rhythms, attuned to both the seen and the unseen. This posture is not passive withdrawal but active receptivity. Trappist monk Thomas Merton, whose writings guide many on the contemplative path, describes awareness thus: "In active contemplation, a man becomes able to live within himself. He learns to be at home with his own thoughts. He becomes to a greater and greater degree independent of exterior supports. His mind is pacified not by passive dependence on things outside himself . . . but by its own constructive activity."[1]

For writers, Merton's insight is revelatory. Contemplation is not about emptying the mind but filling it with holy attention. When we practice this "constructive activity," we begin to see the world as charged with meaning—the slant of afternoon light, the rhythm of a stranger's speech, the ache of a half-remembered dream. These details, perhaps previously overlooked, become entry points for creative work. While I don't resonate with all of Merton's teachings, his insistence on finding God in everything has reshaped how I approach both spirituality and writing. To behold is to recognize that the divine dwells not only in grand gestures but in the mundane moments of daily life.

Sophfronia Scott explores the nexus of contemplation and creativity in *The Seeker and the Monk*, in which Scott engages Thomas Merton's journals to confront contemporary complexities—political unrest, spiritual exhaustion, societal fractures. Scott demonstrates that contemplative practice does not retreat from the world. Rather, it fosters "a kind of engagement with the world" exactly "while having to stand apart from it."[2] For Scott, and for Merton—and maybe for you—the tension between a pull to contemplation and a commitment to address the pressing issues of the day might lead to the protest rally, or to the ballot box. Scott's concern about gun violence found her behind the wheel: "When the Sandy Hook tragedy occurred, I was a licensed school bus driver. I've never been comfortable participating in large demonstrations, but when the first organized protests against gun violence were scheduled to take place in the state capital, I saw something specific I could do, so I drove one of the buses transporting people from my community to the event. I felt I'd made a contribution—and an effective one." But, for writers, a desire to critically engage the current social and political order usually *also*—and often first—leads to the desk. As Scott puts it, writing represents "an authentic way to dissent. . . . I look for opportunities where I can be most effective, doing something specific that only I or few others can do. Usually this means writing."[3]

At its heart, contemplative practice cultivates the kind of deep attention that both writing and social engagement require. Before we can write about injustice, we must first notice it. Before we can capture a moment's beauty, we must first be present to it. Before we can articulate what needs to change, we must first understand what's broken. This is where contemplation serves writers most powerfully—not as an escape from reality but as a lens that brings reality into sharper focus. Whether we're writing poetry about a delicious bowl of stew or essays about climate change, the contemplative practice of sustained attention allows us to see more clearly what needs to be seen, say more precisely what needs to be said. The quiet moments we use for contemplation become the foundation for both our creative work and our engagement with the world's needs.

Lauren Winner reflects on this intersection of contemplation and activism while participating in a Maundy Thursday protest at an immigration detention center. She notes that "protest, like prayer, can become tedious," yet finds hope in the persistence of showing up year after year. "If we are still coming here," she writes, "that means we are still praying." For Winner, contemplation itself becomes a form of resistance, not because it produces immediate results but because it gradually transforms us into people capable of more sustained attention. Through her "halting two decades of prayer—of on-again, off-again prayer, of prayer that is consistent and prayer that is sporadic," she is being made into someone "with the capacity to attend to God and to God's world."[4] This capacity to notice what demands our attention, to see what begs our vision, becomes the foundation for both spiritual and social engagement.

Mystics of all traditions—Christian, Jewish, Sufi; poets, painters, parents tending sleepless children—understand that wonder thrives where certainty ends. A contemplative might find sacred pause in the ritual of morning breath prayers or the act of revising a stubborn paragraph. The key is holding space for the unknown, allowing it to sharpen our gaze rather than blur it.

Behold Through the Examen

But how to keep your gaze focused? Contemplatives understand that the contemplative stance doesn't just arrive. It is cultivated through practices that hone concentration and awaken the practitioner.

One such practice beloved of me is the Ignatian examen. Developed by Ignatius of Loyola in the sixteenth century, the examen is a prayer practice that invites us to review our days with gentle curiosity. As Episcopal priest Rhonda Mawhood Lee summarizes, in the examen, you "look back over" the past day, both to "notice where you experienced God's presence: maybe in a small miracle, like a flower or birdsong; maybe in conversation with an old friend who may know you even better than you know yourself" and to notice "moments where you sinned, did something you regretted, or missed an opportunity to be kind." Jesuits—the monastic community Ignatius of Loyola founded, who first received the examen and in time offered it to the rest of the church—"normally pray the examen twice a day, at noon and at the end of the day. The rest of us can do the examen at any convenient time, usually once a day, and most commonly toward the end of the day (before dinner or before bed)."

To practice the examen, you need a bit of quiet and a pocket of time—maybe ten or twenty minutes. Close your eyes or adopt a blurred gaze at the floor. Inviting whatever holy companion you'd like to join or guide you—I invite the Holy Spirit; you might invite Mary, Hagar, your dead sister, or no one at all—you cast your mind back to the beginning of the day just past. Then walk through the day, noticing, or asking your holy companion to point out to you, those moments named by Lee as moments of "experience[ing] God's presence." Perhaps during a delightful conversation with a neighbor or in the quiet minutes after a gentle rain shower. At the end of your walk through the day, consider offering words of thanks for these holy moments. Then cast your mind back to the beginning of the day again, and take a second stroll, this time noticing those moments of damage, brokenness, or "missed . . . opportunity."[1] Perhaps you might notice a moment of gossip you joined or a creative prompt you dismissed out of fear. After this second stroll, you may want to offer words of regret, repentance, or resolve. You may wish to wrap up the whole experience with a favorite prayer (Saint Ignatius of Loyola's Suspice, for me) or a favorite poem ("How to Triumph like a Girl" by Ada Limon, for me).

The examen can function as a deeper, more meaningful gratitude practice that tunes your soul to behold more goodness and view the divine as Saint Angela of Foligno saw God—as "All Good."[2] The examen helps me see the goodness of my creative life within a larger context. Over time, I've tailored the examen to writing-specific questions, asking not, generically, Where today did I encounter the holy or love my neighbor? but rather: What did I receive through my writing today? What did I offer? Where did I sense belonging? These prompts attune me to patterns—the cycles of rest and productivity, solitude and community—that shape both my art and my spirit. A writer's examen might entail replaying the day's conversations to mine them for dialogue or lingering on an image that insists on becoming a metaphor. The practice trains us to behold not just the extraordinary but the ordinary, knowing that the line that separates the two is thinner than we think.

Contemplation forms a lens. Through it, writers glimpse the interconnectedness of all things—how a childhood memory might inform a character's grief, or how the cadence of a prayer might echo in a poem. To behold is to recognize that every moment, no matter how small, might spark a creative insight while connecting us to the divine, to our readers, and to members of the broader literary community who've wrestled with words before us.

To practice an examen, you might ask yourself the questions below every day for a month. Or every Monday for a year. Or most Fridays. You might develop your own writerly examen questions. Consider:

1. What have I received through my reading and writing?
2. What have I offered others through my writing and creativity?
3. How have I noticed a sense of belonging through my writing and beyond?

4. What new insights have I had that I want to explore through writing?
5. What am I being called to in my writing life and beyond?
6. What do I want more of and what do I want less of in my writing and beyond?
7. Where have I experienced rest and work, writing and not writing, loneliness and belonging, solitude and community, silence and speaking, stillness and movement?
8. Where, in the coming days and weeks, might I experience rest and work, writing and not writing, loneliness and belonging, solitude and community, silence and speaking, stillness and movement?
9. How can I behold more goodness and nourish my creativity?
10. What do I want to remember from this practice? (Jot down a few notes about what emerged through these questions and your answers.)

Behold with Your Body

One of my favorite Bible verses with the word "behold" appears in the King James Version of the Gospel of John when Jesus tells Thomas to behold his physical wounds in response to Thomas's resurrection doubts. Thomas is gathered with the other disciples as Jesus appears in their midst. After his greeting of peace, he says to Thomas, "Reach hither thy finger, and behold my hands; and reach hither thy hand, and thrust it into my side: and be not faithless but believing." Then, with a bold and new belief, Thomas proclaims, "My Lord and my God." Jesus credits the act of seeing for the transformational shift from doubt to faith. "Thomas," Jesus said, "because thou hast seen me, thou hast believed."[1]

Our bodies hold stories waiting to be told. Just as Thomas needed physical contact with Jesus's wounds to fully believe, writers often need embodied awareness to access deeper creative truths. This connection between physical sensation and spiritual insight isn't just metaphorical—it's a pathway to more authentic expression.

What I notice most in this passage is the story's display of sensory and bodily details emphasizing the complex nature of this beholding rather than a simple glimpsing. Jesus's instruction to Thomas to "behold" is coupled with instruction to reach toward and touch multiple wounds with both hands. Thomas's belief trajectory requires a full-body experience of actively and sensorily beholding the embodied presence of the risen Lord. I think writers find, too, that our writing lives are richer when we meet the world with our whole bodies, not just with our minds.

When we write from a place of embodied awareness, we access layers of meaning that purely intellectual approaches might miss. The practice involves noticing physical sensations while writing—the tightness in our shoulders, the rhythm of our breath, the way our posture shifts as we approach difficult topics. Like Thomas reaching out to touch Jesus's wounds, this physical engagement creates a more complete kind of knowing.

The Theological Dictionary of the New Testament tells me the Greek word translated in this verse is *ide*, "which is common in prayers in the sense 'to regard,' 'to observe,'" and sometimes means "to recognize" or "to perceive."[2] I like the idea of seeing with the purpose of recognizing and perceiving. This way of looking requires more than a hurried glance while your mind is elsewhere and your body is ignored. You are looking with more than your eyes to understand in ways that are beyond what the visual and obvious physical appearance might show. There's more happening. (There's *always* more happening, right?) When you behold, your sense of sight leads you to your sense of soul. And since your creative soul is your soul, the act of beholding also expands your imaginative expression.

Integrating bodily awareness with creative practice reminds us that beholding is never only about seeing. It's about engaging with all our senses in service of deeper understanding. The body becomes both witness and vessel for the stories we need to tell, transforming hesitation into conviction and uncertainty into clarity.

When we read, our bodies often know before our minds do. Notice how your jaw clenches during a suspenseful scene, or your breath quickens in response to passionate prose. These physical responses can guide both our reading and our writing. If your throat and chest tighten while reading about a character's grief, what might that tell you about your own sorrow waiting to be processed or told?

This embodied beholding extends beyond the page. When you're sitting in traffic, notice how your body responds to the symphony of horns, engines, and exhaust—the shallow breathing, the urge to move. Or observe how your body softens while watching a monarch butterfly land on a purple coneflower—your shoulders dropping, breath slowing, fingers uncurling. These physical responses aren't merely reactions; they're invitations to deeper perception and richer writing.

It might also be helpful to ponder how your body beholds different environments. Do your muscles relax in a familiar bookstore? Does your spine straighten in a formal meeting or interview? Each physical response provides insight into how we experience and make meaning of our world. Writers who attend to these bodily cues often find their work enriched with sensory details that might otherwise go unnoticed.

You already know one way to begin anything is to begin where you are, right in the middle of whatever's unfolding around you. To grow in your ability to behold, start here. Look around. What do you notice immediately? If you look a bit closer, what else can you see that you missed at first? Then you can continue, throughout a typical day or week, to practice *beholding* more of what you're already accustomed to briefly *noticing*.

How can you behold stillness and silence? Here's one option: Take quiet sips of attention to the present moment for a few minutes at a time. Start small and extend your practice as your comfort with stillness and silence grows.

How can you behold the places in which you live, work, write, and play? Try pausing for brief periods as you move between places and activities. Take six deep breaths before you get out of your car while running errands or after you arrive home from work.

How can you behold the love of God? Some people find that memorizing a soothing line of poetry or Scripture instills good truths in their hearts.

The practice of beholding requires patience and practice, as well as willingness to trust the wisdom that resides in our physical experience while remaining open to where it might lead us. How can your body help you behold more of the natural world? Art? Darkness? Winter? How can you behold the belongings and other good things you receive from your creative practices? What comes to mind when you think about what it means to see with more intention and purpose?

Behold the Ordinary

The film *Paterson* follows one week in the life of a bus driver named Paterson who lives and works in Paterson, New Jersey. Viewers become witnesses of his ordinary, daily routine that includes driving his route, writing poetry in his notebook during breaks, spending evenings with his creative wife, Laura, and their dog Marvin, and visiting a local bar during nighttime walks with Marvin. Paterson is a quiet observer of the city and its people, finding poetry in ordinary moments and conversations while maintaining his simple rhythms.

The film's attention to small details mirrors Paterson's poetic sensibility—the viewer sees morning light fall across Paterson's morning Cheerios and shares in his careful listening to passengers' conversations on the bus. We see him sitting by the Great Falls during lunch breaks, composing poems in his notebook while water cascades nearby, showing how his creativity can emerge from short periods of quiet contemplation in nature. In one touching scene, he encounters a young girl writing her own poetry, highlighting a moment of generous recognition between two artists without either person explicitly identifying as such. The film's cyclical structure, showing Paterson fixing his perpetually tilted mailbox each day (the incessant tilt later revealed to be the work of his dog Marvin), reinforces how meaning can be found in life's recurring patterns.[1]

In *A Whole Life in Twelve Movies*, Kathleen Norris observes how Paterson's disciplined daily schedule has formed a deep inner life. Like a monk who has "stripped his life down to essentials," Paterson creates space for creativity within life's necessary tasks. His dedication to both his job and his art demonstrates how ordinary work can support rather than hinder creative practice. "It is the way he uses his time, and respects other people," Norris writes, "that encourages me to believe that he is a true artist." By embracing simple routines—the same breakfast each morning, the same lunch spot by the falls—Paterson frees his mind to focus on what matters most: his poetry and his relationships. Norris adds, "Paterson writes poetry but isn't seeking attention for that—or anything else. He's a humble man. . . . He doesn't put on airs but takes his responsibilities as a bus driver seriously, arriving on time every morning to make sure his bus is in good condition." One day his bus breaks down, and he makes sure everyone is okay and taken care of. "He's made room to truly care about others and also nourish his deepest desire, which is to write," Norris observes.[2]

If we elevate the act of beholding and imagine it can only occur within the realm of the extraordinary, fewer opportunities for soul looking will present themselves. If we view the quotidian as territory to behold, our souls will never cease their sacred searching. The mundane and ordinary things of life fill most of our days—working, caregiving, cooking, cleaning, resting, enjoying a few hobbies, scrolling through social media, bingeing on TV shows, keeping up with politics and the trash pickup schedule and the to-do lists and the leaky faucet that really should be repaired. What if all these mundanities are opportunities to behold?

ORDINARY was a quarterly fine-art photography magazine, launched in 2016 in Amsterdam. Each issue featured one ordinary object and art that artists from around the world have created using or responding to in whatever way they wish.[3] The first issue of *ORDINARY* contained images of plastic cutlery; the second was full of photographs of a kitchen sponge. One issue included images of a plain white sock. Issue 6 featured photos of air. Yes, air.

Writers can learn from the artists who find endless creative possibilities in a simple white sock or the invisible presence of air. We can also discover richness in life's most basic elements. Each ordinary moment holds potential for insight when we approach it with the same careful attention Paterson brings to his bus route or his morning cereal. This kind of seeing transforms both the observer and the observed.

Sometimes I'm tempted to think I have settled for the ordinary, but that's not accurate. It's not a settling; it's more of an embracing. Well, that's not true either. I often *try* to embrace the ordinary, and some days the embrace sticks.

My friendship with the ordinary began more than sixteen years ago when I was a young mother and came across the small book *The Quotidian Mysteries*, also by Norris.[4] In those early years of wanting to believe the ordinary mattered, I would wake desperate with desire to wrap my arms around an item, idea, or event that was more interesting or exciting than the mundane hours of my ordinary life.

Some days I sat for hours doing not enough, staring at my messy house, dreading making dinner. As much as I found comfort and solace in the ordinary, sometimes it undid me. I couldn't imagine being mired in the mundane forever. Sometimes death seemed like a better option than my ordinary life. Sometimes facing another day just like yesterday stirred in me an anger at God that lingered for weeks. I didn't want to admit any of this to myself, much less reveal it to others, so I limited my interactions with my husband and my two young children, and kept to myself—and inside myself, my quandary about my actual life grew.

But, after I read *The Quotidian Mysteries*, my relationship with the mundane began to change. "We want life to have meaning, we want fulfillment, healing and even ecstasy, but the human paradox is that we find these things by starting where we are, not where we wish we were," Norris writes. "We must look for blessings to come from unlikely, everyday places—out of Galilee, as it were—and not in spectacular events, such as the coming of a comet."[5] With this expanded view of the ordinary, I began to believe good and beautiful things could happen on the living room floor or at the kitchen table. I discovered how to navigate the mundane portions of motherhood without allowing my role as a mother to define everything about me. Embracing the ordinary saved me from much exasperation. It nourished and guided me. I became more satisfied with sitting on my front porch in silence and running errands with my kids. Doing the laundry day after day, again and again, no longer made me want to scream. Moving deeper into the quotidian over the years has also been a teacher for my parenting, a balm for my spiritual life, and a gift for my bipolar disorder diagnosis. After I began writing more seriously, I realized honoring the ordinary would also aid my writing life. Here's the biggest lesson I've learned: An ordinary life can be a calm life, and a calm life can be so much better than the alternative. A calm life that resists busyness provides more opportunities for seeing and inhabiting the present moment. I'm not telling you to stay home and sit on your sofa and stare at your living room walls all day every day. But a calm life can still be a full life.

Honoring the ordinary also helps us resist the pressure to perform. I'm better able to inhabit my writing life and spiritual direction practice without obsessing over platform and follower numbers and client rosters and workshop registrations and book sales and next steps and querying agents and what should the next book be, and all the related writerly things. I'm more willing to believe it's good to be an ordinary writer and an ordinary spiritual director with ordinary book sales. To have an ordinary platform and an ordinary impact on the lives of others. To believe small work can be good work, good work can be small work.

This practice of beholding the ordinary creates a foundation for all creative work. When we glean good things from Paterson's practice of writing poems between bus routes or monks finding meaning in daily tasks, we discover that regular attention to ordinary moments enriches both our writing and our spiritual lives. If we resist the pressure to make everything extraordinary, we often find the extraordinary hiding in plain sight—in morning's growing light, in afternoon shadows, in evening conversations.

The ordinary becomes a doorway to deeper seeing, which in turn leads to richer writing. Crafting poems about breakfast cereal or essays about morning commutes harnesses our intentional attention to everyday life and keeps us grounded in what Mary Oliver points us to—this real, present, available world.[6] It reminds us that meaningful work doesn't require dramatic circumstances or exceptional events. It requires presence to what is already here and honoring the truth, again, that all of life is the writing life.

As we learn to embrace the ordinary moments of life, we discover those moments are gateways to deeper creativity and spiritual awareness. The practice of beholding the mundane transforms not just how we see our daily routines, but how we approach our artistic endeavors. Just as one's life might hold quotidian mysteries, so does one's writing—not every poem we write can be our best or our favorite; not every paragraph can be crystalline. Yet even in these seemingly ordinary moments, something remarkable can emerge. Norris describes this phenomenon as "parturient," a stage of being "in labor, about to produce or come forth with an idea or discovery." She notes, "It always seems that just when daily life seems most unbearable, stretching out before me like a prison sentence, when I seem most dead inside, reduced to mindlessness, bitter tears or both, that what is inmost breaks forth, and I realize that what had seemed 'dead time' was actually a period of gestation."[7]

Behold Art

As a person who is most comfortable with words, beholding visual art helps me connect with myself in ways that are beyond language. This is one reason writers need many forms of art in our lives.

Several years ago, I began sitting with a few large abstract paintings during my frequent visits to the Birmingham Museum of Art. I park in the free lot beside the back entrance and wind my way up the staircase to the main floor. I walk past the gift shop, then turn left. A long corridor takes me to my preferred starting point, the American gallery with five oversized paintings by abstract expressionists. One of my all-time favorites is *Sun Mountain* by Helen Frankenthaler. Measuring at 120.5 inches by 87 inches, this piece makes me feel like I'm inside an alternate, sun-soaked, wordless world, which is always such a relief. When the words disappear, personal and global worries and anxieties dissipate, as well. For ten or fifteen minutes, wars cease and oppression ends. My cholesterol numbers return to normal. A friend's son's illness heals. All that matters is the huge yellow expanse bordered by bits of blue and green with a sliver of raw, blank canvas.

Studies have shown that regular interaction with different forms of visual art improves observational skills, critical thinking, and emotional intelligence. Art also serves as a mirror to our inner world while simultaneously opening windows to new possibilities. Whether through paintings, sculptures, or multimedia installations, art creates a dialogue between the viewer and the creator, fostering a deeper understanding of both the self and the other. This engagement can unlock creative restrictions, inspire new directions in the making of art, and provide fresh insights into artistic practices.

One method of close looking at art was developed by Alfred C. Barnes, founder of the Barnes Foundation in Philadelphia. The Barnes method combines careful observation with critical thinking tools. Rather than rushing to interpretation, the Barnes method begins with detailed attention to visual elements—color, line, light, and space. Observers make initial observations and propose ideas, then test these against the artwork itself, refining or revising their thoughts. This process grounds conclusions in concrete experience: how a painted area conveys solidity or weightlessness, how objects create stability or tension, how elements work together to create the artwork's overall expressive effect. As William M. Perthes, director of adult education at the Barnes Foundation, explains, "A painted area may convey a sense of solidity, three-dimensionality, weightiness, set-ness, and containment. A still life by Cezanne, for instance, may express qualities of precariousness or instability, as objects with the above qualities are set on the inclined plane of a tabletop."[1]

This methodical approach to looking teaches us patience in our encounters with art. Like spiritual direction, it reminds us that first impressions aren't always complete impressions. When we slow down and look closely, art reveals itself gradually, layer by layer. This same careful attention can inform how we approach our own creative work, helping us notice subtle patterns and meanings we might otherwise miss.

When describing her art, Alice Lok Cahana once said, "But of course my art is very silent, because some of the things you want to say, words are not enough, and only the art can talk."[2] These words beautifully express one reason to behold visual art—to do so expands our belonging. Sometimes art shows you more of who you are and what you want. To sit with a painting or sculpture for an extended period, instead of merely glancing, is to receive art's invitation to look closer and see beyond surface appearances while discovering new ways of perceiving both the work and our response to it.

One practice for an art encounter is the practice of *visio divina*—sacred looking, a modification of the age-old Christian prayer practice *lectio divina* (sacred reading). Experiment with *visio divina*, as outlined below. You can practice *visio* with a photo or painting in your home, online, or at a museum, gallery, or other public space.

Before you begin, close your eyes and take a few deep breaths. Notice your breath and your body. Then open your eyes and behold the art or image or object. Try to be fully present to this moment, this place, this work of art. Ask the art to show you what you need to see.

Gaze at the art for at least three minutes, then consider the questions below during a period of silent reflection. You can take notes, if you like. And stay with each image for a total of at least seven minutes. This time of contemplation might be exciting. It might be dull. It might seem like nothing is happening, but sometimes things happen that we can't immediately discern.

1. How do you feel while you're looking at this art?
2. What part of the image or object first captured your attention?
3. How does the painting awaken your senses?
4. How does the painting make you feel less lonely or more lonely?
5. If you were in the image, where would you place yourself?
6. What does the painting want to tell you about yourself, others, and the world around you?
7. What thoughts and feelings does the painting stir in you?
8. What worries arise?
9. What longings surface?
10. What memories come to mind?

In silence, sit with what you have received. Take more notes. Try to come up with a word or phrase that captures your experience of the image or object. If you like, repeat the process with another work of art.

You don't have to limit yourself to visual art. All forms and genres of high art, low art, and in-between art can be attended to with a sacred gaze. Read a book that's on your to-read list or reread one of your favorites. Listen to a newly released album or that playlist you made three summers ago. Watch the popular TV show everyone's talking about or that one movie that always improves your mood.

As you explore various forms of art, remember that each encounter is an opportunity to expand your practice of beholding. Careful attention with time to pause and consider your reactions and responses to what you are beholding becomes a form of creative and spiritual practice, training your eye and heart to see beneath surfaces and beyond first impressions. The way you observe art today—with patience, curiosity, and openness—shapes how you'll notice and perceive the world tomorrow and beyond.

Behold the Outdoors

The outdoors has long been recognized as one of our most profound classrooms and as a source of creative nourishment. Because the natural seasons cyclically repeat, coming and going and returning again, nature offers endless opportunities for contemplation and imaginative insights. From the intricate design of a spider's web to the vast expanse of a starlit sky, the natural world presents us with unending invitations to awe and wonder. The practice of beholding nonhuman creation also connects us to something larger than ourselves. Whether in urban parks or wilderness trails, encounters with the natural world can ground us in the present moment while expanding our creative horizons.

Jesuit priest Gerard Manley Hopkins is one of my favorite nineteenth-century poets. In the introduction to *The Gospel in Gerard Manley Hopkins*, Margaret R. Ellsberg writes, "His greatest greatness, I think, lies in his appropriation of nature to establish religious meaning. Nature, as he idiosyncratically saw it, fastened him to God. He 'instressed' an 'inscape' (pattern), and this act energized him and whatever he looked upon. And though he would spend the final five years of his life plagued by 'fits of sadness so severe they resemble madness,' Hopkins never abandoned the solution he had achieved through his reading of nature's explosive titration with God."[1]

Even in his darkest moments, Hopkins found meaning through careful attention to the natural world. His practice of "instressing"—of discovering and dwelling with the unique essence of things—mirrors what we do as writers when we learn to behold deeply. In his diaries from 1871, Hopkins wrote the following:

> April 22. But such a lovely damasking in the sky as today I never felt before. The blue was charged with same instress, the higher, zenith sky earnest and frowning, lower more light and sweet. High up again, breathing through woolly coats of cloud or on the quains and branches of the flying pieces it was the true exchange of crimson. . . .
>
> May 9. This day and May 11 the bluebells in the little wood between the College and the highroad and in one of the Hurst Green cloughs. In the little wood / opposite the light / they stood in blackish spreads or sheddings like the spots on a snake. The heads are then like thongs and solemn in grain and grape-colour. But in the clough / through the light / they came in falls of sky-colour washing the brows and slacks of the ground with vein-blue. . . . The bluebells in your hand baffle you with their inscape.[2]

As Hopkins was full of wonder through beholding the colors of the sky or a fistful of bluebells, writers can discover profound truth and meaning through patient observation of the ordinary natural world around us.

I saw it yesterday afternoon on my way home after a

dentist appointment: the first lavender cascades of Birmingham's wisteria season. Whenever I see the first wisteria blooms each spring, I become mesmerized by their clusters and the memory of a glorious morning back in 2004 when my daughter, Riley, was fifteen months old. Pretty early on, I'd realized Riley (and later, Riley and Brady) and I had better days together if we took walks around the neighborhood and played outside. During Riley's first spring walking on her own two feet, we ventured out the front door to take a stroll around the block and discovered the wisteria in my neighbor's yard in full bloom. Purple blossoms waterfalled from the top of the tree and hovered just above the sidewalk. The vines were all braggy and showing off their clusters, and we were the delighted audience. My daughter pulled me down our front steps and led me along the sidewalk for closer inspection. After we inhaled the flowers' fragrance and examined the gnarled, woody trunk, I stepped back and watched her giggle and hop then crouch down in silence. She curled herself into the natural fort formed by the shower of branches—a space just her size, a room formed by rain and sunshine and newness and life.

While I was observing her interactions with beauty and nature, it hit me. I knew I was going to be okay. I knew we were going to be okay. In that fragrant moment, my fears about not being enough for her began to dissolve. My daughter didn't need me to pour out more and more of myself to fill her up. I needed to put her in the way of new experiences, ideas, words, encounters. I needed to give her plenty of space to wander, wonder, question, and find her own way in the world. She needed to explore her world and find her own answers, even at this age all wobbly on her legs with skinned knees from the falls still common even though she's been walking for months.

Wisteria—also pinecones, birds, earthworms, pebbles, octopuses—can shift our perspective and realign our priorities. Regular exposure to the nonhuman world reduces stress hormones and improves cognitive function. Time outside enhances creative thinking. When we immerse ourselves in nature, we experience what some scientists call "soft fascination"—a gentle but engaging form of attention that rests and resets our minds. This natural reset can lead to breakthrough moments in our creative work and deeper insights into other areas of life.

Perhaps even more nourishing than being outside with kids is being outside alone. It's a great opportunity to unplug and reconnect with your full self. Taking a walk or sitting on the front stoop with a notebook can help you to disconnect from the digital world and take a respite from various distractions, allowing more time for engagement with your thoughts and creative ponderings. You can let go of everyone else's noise and needs. Nature returns you to your own voice and heart.

Away from the demands of everyday life, you can immerse yourself more fully in your writing with (hopefully) fewer interruptions. Taking a walk in a local park or taking a city center stroll can spark our imagination and ignite our creativity. The sights, sounds, and scents of the outdoors can inspire fresh ideas, unique perspectives, and a sense of wonder. Sitting in the grass in our back yard or another accessible spot can move us past creative resistance toward new sources of inspiration. If you crave a perspective shift, writing in an outdoor setting provides a literal change of scenery, helping you grasp a renewed take on your poem, story, essay, memoir, or journal entry. Open space with a view of the sky offers a broader sense of freedom and expansiveness that enhances your creative process. Calm surroundings with the sounds of birds chirping and leaves rustling are great for introspection and deep work. The next time you're outside for a slow and soulful few minutes, try this practice of quieting that my friend, writer Hallie Waugh, introduced me to: "Be still and listen for the quietest sound you can hear. Then, listen for the next quietest sound, and the next, and so on."[3]

Writing is a deeply human endeavor, and connecting with the natural world reminds us of our place in the more extensive web of life. Being with trees, flowers, or a babbling brook grounds you, brings a sense of calm, and fosters a stronger connection to this wide world. Plants and bodies of water and even piles of dirt can be a source of solace, inspiration, and even metaphorical richness for your writing, as well as a nice break from any depleting difficulties or stressors.

Floral designer Holly Carlisle has a practice she calls Seasonal Sketches that's a great way to engage with the natural world and nurture your creative spirit.[4] Here are some instructions for a simplified version: Start with a walk around your yard, neighborhood, or other outdoor space in which you can cut about fifteen stems of growing things—flowers, grasses, bamboo, shrubbery. Then bring your stems inside and place them in a bucket of water to keep them hydrated. Take fifteen to twenty minutes to play with your stems by creating an arrangement in a vase or other vessel. Experiment with different shapes and modify the energy of your arrangement by clipping stems, rearranging them, adding more stems to the arrangement, or taking some away.

As you become better at seeing the ordinary, art, nature, and beyond, you will be better able to behold your writing and your writing life. You'll discover what to add and what to remove. Which pieces to protect and which pieces to trim away.

Behold Through Rereading

In her book *On Rereading*, Patricia Meyer Spacks explores how returning to texts at different life stages reveals additional layers of meaning and understanding. The practice of rereading forms literary companionships that evolve over time. Spacks notes that rereading is not just about revisiting familiar territory but about discovering how both text and reader have changed. This dynamic relationship encourages more in-depth and nuanced understanding with each encounter.[1] As we establish and reestablish these connections, we learn more about what it means to be human and what it means to simply be.

Sometimes rereading becomes a sacred ritual, a way to honor connections beyond the page. While discussing her favorite books on the *I'd Rather Be Reading* podcast, my friend Carla Jean Whitley shared her tradition of rereading *The Giver* by Lois Lowry on the anniversary of her late sister's death because it was her sister's favorite book. When Carla Jean's book club learned of this practice, they asked to participate, transforming a personal tribute into a shared experience of remembrance and connection.[2] What began as one reader's way of holding space for grief became a communal act of literary belonging and remembering.

When I can't sleep, I turn to *Essays One* by Lydia Davis, particularly "Thirty Recommendations for Good Writing Habits."[3] This essay makes me feel less alone in my writing life, in all of life, in the dark of the night. My continued delight in the author's suggestions affirms that I'm part of a broader literary community full of authors and their thoughts on the writing life.

When Davis describes her note-taking process, I imagine the two of us sitting on opposite ends of a park bench with pens and notebooks, writing down what we notice—perhaps the same people, plants, dogs, ponds. We pause. We take sips of lukewarm coffee from soggy to-go cups. We listen. What sounds can we hear? Birds? Children? Sirens? Wind rustling leaves? We are together but separate in our noticing and noting, and it's a lovely place to be.

I usually fall asleep before the ninth recommendation, "Go to primary sources and go to the great works to learn technique," but that's okay because I have reread this essay many times. I have the bright happy green hardback version of *Essays One* that I bought when it was first published in 2019. I also have the Kindle version because it's one of those books I always need within reach. If I'm home, it's nearby on the bookshelves beside my primary workspace. If I'm out of town or waiting in line at the post office, it's on the Kindle app on my phone. If I'm stuck in traffic or wide awake at two in the morning, I use the audiobook.

I need to have this book within reach the way my son needed his stuffed dog nearby for the first few years of his life. In addition to the comfort it provides, I trust Lydia Davis and figure it's a good practice to keep near those whom one trusts. She's a brilliant writer and thinker who knows a lot is happening in the creative process. She honors the complexities of the craft of writing, as well as the full range of the writing life's joys and despairs. Her stories make me laugh and catch my breath and ask, "How did she just do that?" She never minimizes the writing life's requirements, nor does she attempt to convince me that the writing process requires no wonder or awe.

Davis's *Essays One* was my gateway to rereading, but my practice has grown to include a wide range of treasured books: Toni Morrison's *The Source of Self-Regard*, Vladimir Nabokov's *Speak, Memory*, Jamie Quatro's *Fire Sermon*, Rebecca Solnit's *Orwell's Roses*, Kaveh Akbar's *Martyr!*, and poetry collections by Marie Howe, Ashley M. Jones, Lucille Clifton, Anna Kamienska, and dozens of others.

Rereading develops our critical faculties and strengthens our connection to broader literary traditions. As we go back to texts multiple times, we notice subtle patterns, themes, and techniques that inform our own creative practice. This deepening engagement with literature creates a rich foundation for our own writing, allowing us to draw from a well of carefully observed and thoroughly understood works.

Each return to a beloved text builds new neural pathways and deepens our understanding not just of the work but of our own growth and change. Like visiting old friends, these repeated encounters provide both comfort and challenge, unveiling new layers of meaning with every reading.

Behold Your Own Writing

After a writer who's also a preacher mentioned to me how much pleasure she takes in rereading an essay she's published or a sermon she's just preached, I thought about how rereading your own writing without an editor's eye can be a sacred act of witness. Rereading your own writing as a reader, rather than as the text's author—reading simply to behold what you've done—is an opportunity to return to a familiar landscape with eyes ready to discover brand-new instances of beauty.

When we reread our work leisurely, we often receive surprising gifts. A metaphor that seemed straightforward at first now reveals richer complexities and greater significance. What once appeared as a character's gesture or blouse color now bears an emotional weight we hadn't foreseen. Even journal entries from years ago can illuminate patterns of growth and transformation we couldn't see while living through them. This kind of attentive rereading helps us recognize our own voice and appreciate how it has developed over time.

Like sitting in contemplative silence with a trusted friend, unhurried time with our own words can deepen our sense of creative identity. We notice recurring themes, persistent questions, and evolving perspectives. This practice isn't about ego but about honoring the mysterious ways creativity works through us. Sometimes we write wiser than we know, and only through later rereading do we fully receive the insight our writing self has offered.

The practice of beholding our own writing can also strengthen our creative confidence. When we approach our work with curiosity rather than criticism, we often find moments of unexpected grace—that sentence that sings, the image that resonates, a truth that still holds. This kind of appreciative attention helps counter the inner critic and reminds us why we write in the first place.

Behold Through Remembering

Memory isn't just storage—it's a form of beholding that transforms both past and present. When we remember with intention, giving careful attention to what surfaces, we discover additional levels of significance in familiar experiences. Like light hitting a prism from different angles, each act of remembering reveals fresh facets of what we thought we knew.

Writers practice this kind of beholding when they return to significant moments through their work. Victoria Chang's *Dear Memory* shows how letters to the past can unlock understanding of the present. She writes not just to remember but to consider how memory shapes identity, family history, and cultural inheritance. In a chapter that's addressed to her grandmother, Chang explores the deep human desire to understand origins. "I want to believe we all desire to know how we came to be, who we came from," she writes. "I want to know why my fingers are so long, why my mouth naturally frowns, why my back has chronic pain, why I have freckles all over my nose. Why my mind is so restless."[1] She searches for answers to the questions that explain why we look the way we look, why our bodies move the way they move, why our minds work the way they work.

In *The Art of the Wasted Day*, Patricia Hampl describes these remembered moments as "framed moments" caught in "the sticky amber of recollection." They aren't complete stories but rather thresholds, openings to wider interiors waiting to be explored. These fragments become "construction sites for a palace of values," leading us down "the rabbit hole of thought."

Through daydreaming and remembering, we create spaces for deeper seeing, suggesting that memory isn't just about looking back but about perceiving connections we previously missed. After sharing a memory from childhood—an ice-skating outing during which she declared she'd never have any kids—Hampl reflects on how this half-remembered fragment is only a portion of the larger, blurrier whole: "It is something insubstantial made substantial sheerly by virtue of its indelibility. A vignette shifts the mind away from storytelling into speculation. Why, why? A bit of narrative sand irritating itself into a pearl of thought. An *essai* in the making. . . . And this, on the smooth surface of our home ice, is my first. But is it art? It is not. It's life. That's all, the sand-grit that works its way under the shell of the self. There are so many shifting sands, glinting in the winter light, moments that make a life, though not, alas, a story."[2]

Hampl's childhood memory of ice skating is not a complete story, but it's still valuable—indeed, it's valuable in part because it's partial, carving out space for her to make meaning at the rough edge where memory ends. These sticky moments and vignettes that we remember and reremember often expose themselves as pivotal markers of identity long after they occur. Memories we thought were fully processed still hold surprises. A childhood scene suddenly reveals new significance.

A conversation from years ago offers unexpected insight into current struggles. This kind of beholding through memory requires both attention and patience. And it sometimes requires a willingness to reacquaint ourselves with pasts it has previously served us not to remember.

The practice of beholding through remembering invites us to notice not just what we remember but how we remember. What details surface first? What sensory experiences linger? What emotions arise? These observations often lead to a richer understanding of both past and present, helping us see patterns and meanings we might otherwise miss.

Working with memory requires trust, believing that what needs to surface will surface in its own time. When we approach our memories with this kind of contemplative attention, they become not just records of the past but guideposts for the future, showing us who we're becoming even as they remind us who we've been.

What do you want to remember?

Behold Through Reflection

Every significant writing experience and spiritual encounter deserves to be witnessed and integrated through intentional reflection. Whether you've just completed a weekend workshop, emerged from a weeklong retreat, finished writing a memoir, or are getting closer to being done reading this book, taking time to reflect on what you've learned and received allows you to savor insights that might otherwise be lost. We are usually too quick to move on to the next thing without pausing to ponder what we just wrapped up. Some experiences might need a half hour or maybe even a few slow days of reflection to uncover their underlying meanings like letting tea steep to release its full flavor.

A full year passed before Angela of Foligno, a Franciscan penitent who lived in the latter part of the thirteenth century, began an intense season of reflection about a spiritual experience with a scribe and collaborator called "Brother A" in her writings.[1] Brother A had witnessed Angela's intense public display of grief during her pilgrimage to the Basilica of Saint Francis when she lost profound consolation and intimate presence of the Trinity and transitioned into the difficulty of desolation and divine absence. Angela caused such an emotional disturbance in the basilica that the friar asked her to leave and return to Foligno. Months later, when Brother A was reassigned to Foligno, he tracked down Angela and asked her to explain what had caused the shrieks and cries during her time in Assisi. Thus began Angela's process of sustained reflection, as well as a collaboration with Brother A, who served as her scribe and confidant. The writings eventually made their way to various communities and individuals, providing spiritual nourishment to many. According to Diane V. Tomkinson, "Angela became a revered spiritual teacher for other friars and penitents who gathered around her in the decade or so prior to her death in 1309."

Her words are still studied today, and several people have noted the spiral nature of her prayers and overall journey. Tomkinson observes, "The intrinsic spiral pattern of Angela's prayer offers a vision of Christian spirituality in which loving relationship with God cannot be separated from right relationship with all other creatures, each of which is valued as a particular expression of the infinite All Good." Brother A's curiosity and questions prompted Angela to reflect and record her spiritual insights that have encouraged many throughout several generations. The account of her mystical prayers and intimate divine encounters provides a "distinctive spirituality of communion that offers a fruitful pattern for contemporary pilgrims."[2]

While your reflections may not become anything that will benefit scores of Christians over multiple generations, the practice of reflection helps us behold what we've learned and notice patterns in our creative process and spiritual journey. It prepares us to celebrate accomplishments and acknowledge disappointments. Through careful consideration, we can determine how to carry forward what serves us and release what doesn't.

Here's a guided practice to help you reflect on your writing and spiritual experiences: Begin with three deep breaths and two minutes of silence. This transition helps you shift from doing to being, creating space to notice what wants to be seen. Set a timer if it helps you fully settle into the silence.

Then, working with these prompts, make four lists. Take about three minutes with each list:

- What people, places, things, art, and ideas from this writing experience helped you belong more fully to yourself? Be specific about moments of connection and insight.
- What elements particularly nourished your creative practice or spiritual growth? Consider both expected and unexpected sources of inspiration.
- What aspects of this experience will you miss? This question helps identify what you might want to incorporate into your typical days.
- Looking ahead, what do you want more of in your writing and spiritual life? What do you want less of?

After making your lists, take time to notice how you're feeling in your body, mind, and soul. What thoughts are arising? Journal freely about whatever surfaces.

The final step is to think about how to integrate what you've learned into your writing life. Perhaps you'll establish new rituals based on what worked well during a retreat. Maybe you'll seek out more opportunities for the kind of feedback that proved helpful in a workshop. Or you might create regular spaces for the types of spiritual practices that deepened your work during a project.

Share your insights with someone who understands your writing life—a friend, mentor, spiritual director, or fellow writer. Similar to Angela of Foligno capturing the details of her pilgrimage experiences with the help of a scribe, speaking our reflections aloud to an attentive soul often enhances memories of what we've learned and strengthens our commitment to any changes we want to make.

Close your time of reflection with a few deep breaths, allowing yourself to transition mindfully back into your regular rhythms while carrying forward what you've discovered.

Behold Through Retreats

Going on short retreats can be a real boon to the writing life, providing longer periods of time to read the books that have been piling up, begin writing a new piece or wrap up an existing project, and practice beholding in some of the ways mentioned above. If you've experienced a significant change like starting a different job, completing a recent move, or having a new child, intentionality retreating—even for an hour a week—can prevent a creativity breakdown.

The crux of a writing retreat involves ignoring all nonemergency external demands while dedicating time to behold important aspects of your writing life (so whenever you're about to retreat, you get to tell everyone and everything, "I'll be unavailable for the next four (or eight or one and a half hours").

In episode 7 of the TV show *Tiny Beautiful*, the protagonist, Clare Pierce, attends a writing retreat with her best friend, Amy. When Clare hops in the passenger seat of Amy's car, she's retreating from strained relationships with her husband and teenage daughter, work difficulties and recent disciplinary actions due to disturbing misconduct, haunting memories about her past and her dead mother, in-laws that definitely know something's wrong while she keeps trying to make everyone think nothing's wrong, regrets about her writing life and how she skips church every Sunday to write but never actually writes, and all of the daily responsibilities, interruptions, and obligations that typically require too much of her time and attention.

While Clare is buckling her seatbelt and settling in for the road trip, Amy begins to rattle off a list of snacks for the road trip and retreat. "So, I got jerky. I got CBD lollies . . ." When Clare interrupts with a loud sigh and visible signs of distress, Amy stops and asks what's wrong. Clare gives a response that many of us could give to the same question just about any time any day: "Nothing. Everything. I don't know." She adds, "Let's just go."[1] As they drive away from Clare's home and family, viewers might recall the question she asked in a previous episode: "How did I get so far from the person I wanted to be?"[2]

Making a retreat paradoxically pulls you out of the things that constitute the warp and woof of your life to help you draw nearer to the person you want to be. Some of the things you can put on hold during solo writing retreats include communications from family and friends, work obligations, to-do lists, household chores, news reports, political turmoil, and the latest natural disaster updates. While we retreat *from* things that get in the way of writing, reading, and our preferred nourishing rhythms, we move *toward* increased clarity around the condition of our works-in-progress and greater understanding of a healthier creative life overall.

When I asked a writer friend to describe what it's like for her to have a retreat, she described a three-day, almost entirely silent retreat she had at her home a couple of winters ago. She shared the key actions and choices that made her three-day at-home retreat an actual retreat. First, she found herself emotionally and mentally obsessing about a pressing emotional burden in the two days before the retreat started. On the first evening of the retreat, she wrote a letter about the situation that was causing so much mental and emotional anguish and walked it down the street to a blue mailbox. "I mailed the letter, and the obsession returned after the retreat. But the act of writing and mailing that letter did actually get the situation out of my head for the needed forty-eight hours. It was helpful to have a physical ritual action of expurgation at the start of the retreat." Second, she told all the people that she talked to regularly that she was having this silent retreat. "People knew not to expect to hear from me, which was crucial." Finally, she used a specific room in her home for prayer. "I have a more formal living room, which I don't use much. That became the room in which I did my dedicated praying."

I love that my friend knows what she needs for her retreats to feel like retreats. Maybe her insight will help you plan your next solo writing retreat. What do you need to put aside before your retreat starts? What embodied ritual can be your signal that it's time for a retreat? What room or corner could you set for your core retreat activities?

Using a retreat practice to examine aspects of your creative process and honor your writerly needs will also enhance nonretreat days. If you begin to incorporate a few favorite retreat elements throughout your typical days and weeks, your retreats will inform the rest of your life as you navigate patterns of work and rest, energy and lethargy, inspiration and suppression. If you enjoy having large amounts of time free from interruptions during retreats, how can you incorporate similar smaller pockets of time on nonretreat days? If you appreciate the unhurried pace during retreats, which adjustments will invite you into more slowness more often? As you retreat, notice the relaxing sensations in your body, the stillness of your mind, and the fullness of your soul. Then experiment with different ways to re-create those experiences on a smaller scale on those random Tuesday evenings when you realize you happen to have an extra twenty minutes to yourself.

One simple way to have more retreat time is to plan regular four-hour solo writing retreats, maybe once a month. If you don't have a four-hour window of time for a monthly retreat, I encourage you to wonder about how you could preserve more blank space on your calendar and in your life. What needs to change? What can you let go of? What can you do less often? When you're ready to schedule a four-hour solo writing retreat, here are some instructions to get you started.

Plan: Pick a date, a time, and a place. If possible, make sure no one will interrupt you during your retreat unless there's an emergency. (If you pray, pray for no emergencies. For additional reinforcement, ask a friend to pray for you to have no emergencies.) Block out your retreat time on your calendar and tell those who may need you that you will be unavailable. Arrange child care, time off from work, delegate household duties. Comb through your collection of pens, stationery, mugs, and consider setting one or two special items aside for retreating. If it's within your budget, consider splurging on one new pen or a new notebook. There's value in setting apart certain objects for special retreat use. Using these special items is one way to let your body, mind, and soul know it's retreat time.

Prepare: Create a retreat schedule to suit your needs. Fill a four-hour plan with nourishing rhythms in twenty- or thirty-minute increments. Have an open mind, heart, and soul while preparing your retreat schedule. During your retreat, you may need to make some adjustments, and that's okay! It's better to prepare and make some tweaks than to show up without any preparation. If you pray, set aside a few minutes each day leading up to your retreat for prayer. Ask God to show you what you need to see more clearly, help you discover what you desire most, enable you to determine what you can let go of and what you can hold on to before, during, and after your retreat.

Retreat: Using your retreat guide, a timer, and plenty of beverages and snacks, enjoy your retreat! Your timer is your friend, but it can also be an enemy. Give your attention to what you need and want in the moment and make guilt-free adjustments to your solo writing retreat schedule as your retreat unfolds. Throughout your retreat, receive what this particular retreat has for you on this particular day. Try to let go of expectations or needing a specific outcome. Your schedule might shift to allow for an extended writing session that's flowing well, even if it means shortening your planned reading time. Or you may decide to take a longer walk than planned because your body and mind need more movement. If your writing isn't going well, it might be good to allocate extra time to reading or follow an unexpected creative impulse that wasn't on your schedule. Remember: The schedule serves you, not the other way around. True retreat time honors the organic rhythms of creativity and rest, allowing space for both structure and spontaneity.

Receive: Notice the good things and hard things you receive during and after your retreat. It might be helpful to journal or keep a simple list throughout your retreat.

Reflect and Respond: Set aside a few minutes each day for three days after your retreat to sit with and answer these three questions: What did I receive in my retreat for which I am grateful? How can I incorporate one element of my recent solo writing retreat in my regular daily and weekly rhythms? When do I need to have my next solo writing retreat? I recommend asking yourself these questions for three days following your retreat because it may take some time to settle into the answers. Don't rush it.

Retreat days are rarer than I prefer. Work, family obligations, and other responsibilities usually require large portions of my energy and attention. But sometimes I can sneak in a mini-retreat. When I'm able to do so, I read, write, walk, and pray for ten minutes each and call it a forty-minute micro solo writing retreat because using retreat language puts my desires first, dismisses everything else for brief periods, honors my favorite nourishing rhythms, and increases my chances of witnessing wonder and encountering delight.[3]

Behold Through Travel

Another way to expand your creative process and have extra opportunities for beholding is to travel like a writer, trusting that good things and creative stimulation await you at your destination and along any roads that carry you there. This approach to travel with an emphasis on closer looking transforms a quick road trip into a form of delightful play.

The next time you travel, try to add at least one solo writing retreat to the itinerary. It needn't be expensive. If you have time to plan before your departure, research historical markers, local diners, independent bookstores, public libraries, walking trails, prayer labyrinths, and tea shops. Be on the lookout for places and events that are aligned with your quirky interests too. I love cemeteries and try my best to explore them whenever I travel. What do you love?

If one bit of research seems to stand out above the rest, if the vibes of a local record shop are a sort of siren singing a melody to your soul, start there. After you arrive, check out the surrounding area and any various options for next steps, then let things unfold and wait and see what will happen next.

When you travel, carve out time for a bookstore or library in the town you're visiting. Once there, track down the "staff recommendations" and "local interest" sections.

Scope the shop for a bookseller who doesn't look too busy and ask for their recommendations. Sometimes I ask questions like "What have your regulars have been buying?" "Which memoirs have been your best sellers this year?" "What about YA?" "Can you recommend a book that will tell me about local history or a book by a local author?" Then I add a note to my wish list or purchase a few books because books are good things to spend money on if you have some money to spend. And buying books with connections to a place and its people will help you feel less alone in this world, which is always a good outcome.

Then go outside, look both ways, and see what's nearby. Once, when I was in Albany, New York, there was a famous cheesecake bakery right next to the used bookstore I had scouted out during a layover in Atlanta earlier that day. So, with three new-used novels and a new-used history of the Hudson Valley in my tote bag, I bought a piece of chocolate cheesecake. Then I took a walk around the block. I passed a Mexican restaurant with a lovely outdoor seating area to which I returned for an early dinner. It was mid-October and the weather was perfect. Trees were all around, and it was peak leaf season, so I was surrounded by more beauty than a person deserves. My server recommended their homemade corn soup and said it was the absolute best. I went with her recommendation and marveled at the bowl placed before me. The soup arrived steaming in an earthenware bowl, its velvety surface dotted with Mexican *crema* and chopped, fresh cilantro. Each spoonful held the sweet essence of yellow corn and the subtle smokiness of roasted poblanos. As the afternoon turned to dusk, strings of twinkling lights brightened the faces of diners taking advantage of happy hour margaritas. I ate my soup, flipped through my books, added about seven hundred words to an essay, and enjoyed my slice of famous Dutch chocolate cheesecake.

Of course, taking a retreat when traveling with your family or other people will require more preparation. It's a good idea to have conversations with everyone affected ahead of time. Try saying something like this to your partner: "While we're at your mother's for Christmas, I'd love to have a four-hour solo writing retreat. Is that okay? I want to go by that fantastic bookstore downtown and write at the café a few blocks away, the one that overlooks the river. Can you ask your mom if she can help you with the kids while I'm gone? I can leave early on Saturday morning and be back by noon." And try saying something like this to your children: "While we're at your grandma's, I'm going to have a solo writing retreat on Saturday morning. I'm excited to have some time to write while you hang out with Grandma. Maybe she'll make your favorite cinnamon toast."

Traveling—and traveling with others—can certainly be more complicated than what's described here. But I encourage you to have a creative mind-set. How can you incorporate some solo writing retreats into your travel plans, even if only a forty-minute micro retreat? Maybe you'll need to wake early one morning to fit in a retreat. Maybe four hours isn't doable. Take an hour or two for yourself instead of four. But practice making more time for your writing while traveling and telling others how they can support you.

Behold Anyway

From time to time our efforts to behold fail. A couple of years ago I checked on a friend one Sunday evening after what was supposed to be a much-needed weekend solo writing retreat—her first opportunity for a retreat since the pandemic. She's a poet who was coming out of a rough season and was looking forward to a restful weekend with plenty of spaciousness for reflection and processing the previous several months. "Well," she replied. "It was more of a solo crying retreat."

It happens.

You can plan a perfect retreat getaway with a beautiful schedule that includes all your favorite nourishing rhythms and a detailed agenda, only to show up to your retreat space and watch it all fall apart. While the disruption of plans can be disappointing, I encourage writers (and myself!) to hold on loosely to our perfect solo writing retreat guides and schedules. Sometimes we don't know what our bodies, minds, and souls need until we walk out onto the verdant field full of open green space staring back at us. My friend wanted to read, write, and hang out in hip cafés sipping seasonal lattes all day and drinkable wines all night, but what she needed was to stay in the hotel room and weep.

One way to mitigate the negative feelings about a retreat or reflection session that doesn't go the way you want it to go for whatever reason and give yourself good things anyway is to see the situation more clearly with curiosity. If you are surprised to discover you are on a solo crying retreat or a solo sleeping session instead of the solo writing retreat or two-hour reflection session you planned and imagined, here are some questions to stir your curiosity: I wonder why my body, mind, and soul need this instead of what I planned? How can I care for myself right now? What am I disappointed about specifically? Why am I angry? Why am I sad? What did I miss—why did I not realize I needed this instead of what I planned? What can I learn from this situation?

You don't need to know the answers to those questions. You don't need to journal or pray or take more than a moment with each one. Sometimes simply asking questions helps. Becoming a more curious and compassionate observer provides a bit of distance from the difficult emotions, which can be quite helpful when things aren't going the way you thought they would go. When you have the energy, desire, and time to ponder the questions above (or other questions that are a better fit!), take some time to explore the answers and insights in ways that seem appropriate at that moment. Determine when you might have a chance to try again in the coming weeks or months. Schedule some fifteen-minute chunks of reading and writing. See if a friend or family member can help with other tasks and responsibilities so you can rest. Cross a few unnecessary things off your to-do list. Add more nourishing rhythms. What do you need more of? What do you want less of? What sounds comforting? What sounds inspiring?

Bestow

I have found that among its other benefits, giving liberates the soul of the giver.

—Maya Angelou

Much like "beholding" is a multifaceted way of seeing, "bestowing" is a more complex view of giving. True gifts come from a place of abundance rather than scarcity, generosity rather than obligation. To bestow is to offer what has been given to you, placing your gifts where they might nourish others. Like nature bestowing its abundance—sun offering light, flowers sharing nectar, clouds releasing rain—the act of bestowing flows from fullness rather than obligation.

The word's root in "stow"—meaning "place" or "location"[1]—reminds us that bestowing requires discernment about where and how to share our gifts. Sometimes we bestow through published works, sometimes through letters to friends, sometimes through journal entries that may never be read. Each placement carries its own purpose, its own potential for transformation.

Writers bestow through words, stories, and the careful placement of language that helps others feel less alone. We take what we've received and transform them into gifts for readers we may never meet. We offer our experiences. We express our insights. We give the shimmers of our imagination. The act of bestowing changes both the giver and the receiver, creating connections across time and space.

In spiritual direction, we learn that bestowing often happens in unexpected ways. A moment of vulnerability in a writing group becomes a gracious present of permission for others to be authentic. A piece written from grief offers comfort to someone facing similar loss. Even our struggles, when shared honestly and authentically, can bestow hope or understanding or simply the knowledge that none of us walks alone. To bestow is to trust that your words, placed with intention and given with love, will find their way to those who need them most. Like starlight traveling through darkness, they illuminate paths we might never see with our own eyes but trust in, nonetheless.

Bestow Through Both Receipt and Offering

Bestowing—offering—is often one step in a generous and generative dance: receive and offer, receive and offer. This is true in the spiritual life (I think of the eucharistic prayer, in which we speak of "offering to you [God], from the gifts you have given us, this bread and this cup"). And it is true in the writing life. I can bestow because of how richly I have received.

Perhaps the nonhuman world of plants and animals and earth also experiences receipt and bestowal as a kind of dance. Winter receives autumn's fallen leaves that decompose to enrich the soil with nutrients. Cold temperatures trigger dormancy in plants, allowing them to store energy. Frozen soil improves soil structure through freeze-thaw cycles that break up clay particles. Winter also bestows insulating snow cover that protects dormant plants and provides moisture for the earth's flora. Spring receives winter's stored moisture and improved soil structure, while lengthening days trigger hormonal changes in plants. Melting snow and ice release nutrients and water, bestowing new growth that will feed summer's abundance. Summer receives benefits from spring's foundation to spur growth and pollinator activity. Longer days and warmer temperatures aid photosynthesis, and plants convert spring's moisture into biomass. Summer's abundance includes mature fruits, seeds, and energy stores for autumn processes. The season of autumn receives summer's accumulated energy in plants. Shorter days trigger preparation for dormancy, and plants push nutrients from leaves to the roots. Autumn gifts fallen leaves and organic matter that ultimately nourish winter's soil.

The lines between the seasons blur because there's so much activity in both directions—give and receive, give and receive. The boundaries between seasons are incredibly fluid in the soil, where microorganisms work year-round, breaking down organic matter, fixing nitrogen, and maintaining the underground networks that connect plants. This continuous cycle of receiving and giving mirrors the creative process, where periods of apparent dormancy often enable later flourishing, where nourishment leads to depletion and depletion invites one to nourishment, where curiosity sparks new ideas that generate additional curiosities, where beholding flows into bestowing, and vice versa.

The writing life, too, is marked by constant gift exchange with natural patterns of giving and receiving, each action creating conditions for the other. We receive inspiration from reading and bestow our own words through writing. We gather energy in solitude and share it in community. We take in feedback from trusted readers and offer responses to others' work. We absorb experiences and transform them into stories. We collect fragments of language and craft them into poems or essays. We receive guidance from mentors and later bestow that wisdom to less experienced writers. Even in our daily practice, we give our attention to the page and receive what emerges. We offer our presence to difficult emotions and receive deeper understanding. We give time to revision and receive clarity. These exchanges happen simultaneously and cyclically—the act of giving becomes its own form of receiving, while receiving compels us to give.

Lewis Hyde's *The Gift* explores the cyclical nature of gifts. He notes that the term "bestow" carries connotations of receiving and giving simultaneously, and that the word implies that the givers and receivers—and perhaps the gift itself—experience transformation as the bestowed item or idea is passed on. Hyde describes this process in his discussion of the creative process and a mind-set of abundance:

> So long as the gift is not withheld, the creative spirit will remain a stranger to the economics of scarcity. Salmon, forest birds, poetry, symphonies, or Kula shells, the gift is not used up in use. To have painted a painting does not empty the vessel out of which the paintings come. On the contrary, it is the talent which is not in use that is lost or atrophies, and to bestow one of our creations is the surest way to invoke the next. There is an instructive series of gifts in the *Homeric Hymn to Hermes*. Hermes invents the first musical instrument, the lyre, and gives it to his brother, Apollo, whereupon he is immediately inspired to invent a second musical instrument, the pipes. The implication is that giving the first creation away makes the second one possible. Bestowal creates

> that empty place into which new energy may flow. The alternative is petrifaction, writer's block, "the flow of life backed up."[1]

Hyde's insight that gifts create an "empty place into which new energy may flow" illuminates why bestowing is essential to the creative cycle and suggests how a more consistent writing practice exactly stimulates new ideas for things to write about. When we withhold our gifts—whether through fear, perfectionism, or a sense of scarcity—we risk becoming stuck in what Hyde calls "petrifaction."[2] But when we are writing and bestowing our work generously, we participate in an ancient pattern of emptying and filling, receiving and giving, that keeps creativity flowing.

Bestow Through Words and Objects

Writers naturally gravitate toward bestowing gifts of words because we love words, and we grasp their power to transform, comfort, and connect. We know how a single line of poetry or a handwritten note can brighten a dull day and how a well-timed quotation might offer the exact guidance needed. When we share words with intention, we're creating moments of recognition and understanding.

Objects, too, can be meaningful gifts when chosen with careful attention to what matters to the recipient. A writer might send a friend a small brass key she found in an antique shop because she remembered a conversation they'd had about unlocking creativity. Another may send her mentor a packet of lavender seeds to honor his story about his grandmother's garden. These aren't expensive or elaborate gifts, but they are evidence of seeing, knowing, being attentive to another person.

This kind of bestowing flows naturally from the practice of beholding. When we notice what moves people, what interests them, what brings them joy or comfort, we can respond with gifts that acknowledge these deeper currents in their lives. Sometimes that means sharing precisely the right words at the right moment in a letter or through a special book gift. Other times it means finding or creating an object that represents something that matters to them—an unusual shell or piece of glass for the beach walker, a vintage fountain pen or stationery for the letter writer.

Whether through words or objects, these acts of bestowing say: I know what moves you. I've been paying attention. In this way, the practice of bestowing becomes another expression of the writer's fundamental work: witnessing and honoring the details that make each life unique.

Consider the last time you received the perfect words for a particular moment. Maybe it was a friend texting a poem by your favorite poet just when you felt most disconnected from your creativity. Perhaps it was finding an encouraging note tucked into a book someone lent you. Or maybe it was opening a letter or an email that helped you feel less alone in your struggles.

And sometimes writers bestow words and objects together. Emily Dickinson sent her poems to more than forty correspondents along with carefully chosen gifts that amplified her words' meaning. She would tuck a dead bee into an envelope with verses about "idleness and Spring" for her young nephew, or send a cricket wrapped in paper alongside what she called "My Cricket" poem. She once sent a cake and flowers to Nelly Sweetzer with a line of poetry: "Blossoms will run away, cakes reign but a day, but memory, like melody, is pink eternally."[1] These weren't mere accompaniments—they were transformative acts that turned ordinary objects into vessels of meaning. Dickinson sent her beloveds pieces of her world—poems, as well as roses from her garden, pressed dandelions tied with red ribbon, even maple sugar with a playful note warning the recipient not to "bite the Parish, by mistake, though you may be tempted." Daniel Manheim suggests that Dickinson's true gift wasn't the material object itself, but rather how her creative spirit transformed simple items into something extraordinary through the addition of verse.[2]

During a recent visit to Eudora Welty's house in Jackson, Mississippi, I noticed two things: the stacks of books everywhere and the gifts. A swan's feather Welty received from a friend because of her love for the poem "The Wild Swans at Coole" by William Butler Yeats. A few excellent crayon drawings from the son of another favorite poet. Letters from readers and colleagues with words full of love and admiration. Before I left, I stopped by the gift shop to make a few purchases, including a book of Welty's writings about her garden for a writer friend who's not much of a gardener but enjoys reading about others' gardens. A week later, I received a note in return; give, and receive; give, and receive.

Bestow Through Presence

This cycle of giving and receiving manifests in our regular writing practice, where even the simplest act of showing up to write becomes a gift we both give and receive—even if no one reads what we've written.

Consider a Saturday morning. You wake early. It's raining, and you don't have to do anything or be anywhere until after lunch. You want to write, but you haven't written anything in weeks. For some reason, it feels easier to stay in bed and think about all the ways you aren't doing the writing you want to do. Inertia is real. But inertia can also shift. You decide to go for it through the easiest entrance available to you. Because your most consistent practice ever since you read Julia Cameron's *The Artist's Way*[1] is morning pages, you decide to start there. And you tell yourself you can do one page instead of three. After you pick up your pen, the words fall to the page like a cascading waterfall. A rush of words and ideas. No time to worry about punctuation or spelling. The point is the writing. You are doing it. It's not a poem that you can submit to journals for others to read. Perhaps you'll start a poem tomorrow. But you wrote new words. That's what matters.

When we engage consistently with our writing practice, we develop a particular kind of attention—one that is more aware of subtle shifts in mood, finds meaning in small gestures, and remains present to what's unfolding. This heightened sensitivity, cultivated through the act of writing, becomes a gift we can offer others. Just as we learn to attend carefully to details, metaphors, and underlying meanings in our writing, we become better equipped to attend to the people in our lives. This morning's writing practice opened something in you—not just creativity, but capacity. Because you showed up for your writing, you're now better equipped to show up for others.

When you meet your friend for coffee later that afternoon, she's sipping her bold brew but not saying much. She keeps stirring her drink with a spoon even though she hasn't added any cream or sweetener. The swooshing around and around is loud enough to muffle the sound of whatever song is playing on the café's sound system, but her silence is even louder.

You've tried to get the conversation going with a few open-ended questions, but she's not biting. She's obviously down about something. Bothered? Sad? You consider asking more questions about whatever might be going on. To see if she wants to talk it out. But you check in with yourself first. Do you have energy for a difficult conversation? Can you give her the gift of your presence? Can you hold space for whatever she might reveal? You sense that the answer to these questions is a resounding yes—in fact, you feel better than you have in weeks. You're less angsty. There's not as much of that fear or shame that plagues you when you go too long without writing.

You wonder if your morning pages session earlier that day formed you to be the friend you want to be right now. Maybe. Maybe not. Probably so. It's hard to separate your morning pages experience from your desire to give your friend the gift of your attention. Because you belonged to yourself, became more of yourself, and beheld good things through your morning pages exercise, you are better prepared to be a good friend. Writing forms us to be more of our full selves, so we have more of a self to bestow.

The same skills that help us craft meaningful sentences—patience, careful observation, willingness to sit with uncertainty—also help us be present with others. When we write regularly, we strengthen our capacity to notice, listen, and hold space for complexity. The morning's writing session didn't just produce words on a page; it cultivated a quality of attention that now allows you to sit with your friend's silence, to wonder about the stirring spoon, to remain near without rushing to fill the space with words.

One of my favorite literary examples of gift giving occurs in *The Book Thief* by Markus Zusak. Max, the young Jewish man hiding in the basement of Liesel Meminger's foster family's house, makes her a homemade book by adding his own drawings and writings over pages taken from *Mein Kampf*. This gift Liesel receives, *The Standover Man*, is a beautiful offering of writing and art that overwrites a story of evil with a story of friendship. The book strengthens the existing relational connections between an adult and a child who share a season of suffering, and it ultimately saves Liesel's life because she's in the basement reading her cherished gift during the bombing of Himmel Street. *The Book Thief*'s readers are invited to imagine how we have received—and how we might replicate—similar generosities.[2]

In "Literacy and Power of Words in Markus Zusak's The Book Thief," Ancy Thresia N K examines how *The Book Thief* celebrates the power of words and their ability to provide "a sense of security, power and expression" amid horrible suffering: "Liesel's ability to read excels with home school spelling bees in the basement where the Hubermanns will soon house a Jew. Not only does Liesel's newfound understanding of reading help her to understand the society around her but helps her form a life changing bond with Max Vadenburg, the Jew in the basement with daily weather reports and long nights of reading to each other." Ancy Thresia N K emphasizes that, in *The Book Thief*, words "need not to be spoken, for most of the characters in the novel express themselves through written works such as journals, biographies, etc. This is finally shown through Liesel's bibliography dictating her life from the moment her journey began."[3] In Max's gift to Liesel, we see how bestowing through writing becomes an act of profound presence with a generous offering that reaches beyond the words on a page. The gift includes his whole self, his attention, his story, his way of seeing the world. The handmade book represents a beautiful bestowal: the gift of being seen and understood by another.

The power of bestowing creative gifts extends beyond fictional examples into our real writing lives. When we write with full presence, we give readers more than just information or entertainment—we offer them our unique way of experiencing and making sense of the world. This bestowal of presence happens whether we're crafting fiction, memoir, or poetry. Each thoughtfully constructed scene and honest exploration of difficult truth becomes a way of saying to our readers: "I am here with you in this moment, sharing not just my thoughts but this particular way of being in the world." Like sitting in silence with a troubled friend, this kind of presence requires courage, vulnerability, and trust in the transformative power of showing up to the page.

A former spiritual director helped me learn this lesson when I was writing my first book. I was worried about how my book would sell and if it would receive positive reviews. I wondered how people would view me after reading honest accounts about my mental health, my marriage and other relationships, and my spiritual-formation experiences. Susan listened patiently as I rattled off my list of concerns. Then she encouraged me to turn my attention to my readers and what I want to offer them. "Don't focus too much on yourself and what you want from this experience. Think about what you want to give your readers. Let that be your primary guidance and motivation while writing this book." As I began to contemplate the good things I wanted readers to receive, my anxiety dissipated. Returning to writing as a form of offering continues to help me let go of the self-consumption that can creep into the writing—and publishing—life. What gifts do you want to bestow on your readers?

Bestow Through Story

Books matter because stories are fundamental to human survival and flourishing. Since humanity's beginning, every generation has recognized stories' power to help us learn vital lessons, preserve cultural wisdom, and puzzle answers to knotty questions. Through stories, we grow our belongings and process our personal and collective experiences, finding that profound relief of recognition: "Oh, I'm not the only one who feels this way."

One of my favorite books about narrative structure and story is Steven Pressfield's *The Artist's Journey*. In the first few pages, readers learn some of Pressfield's own story—he experienced what he calls his "all is lost moment" when he was in his midtwenties working as an advertising executive, yet he came to an "epiphanal moment" when he found a way forward out of despair.[1] That epiphanal moment arrived when he dragged out his ancient typewriter. "For two hours I made myself sit there, torturing out some trash that I chucked immediately into the shitcan." After this unpleasant writing session, he put the machine away and went back to the kitchen, where ten days of dirty dishes sat. He realized he finally had enough energy to wash them. "The warm water felt pretty good," Pressfield noticed. "The soap and sponge were doing their thing. A pile of clean plates began rising in the drying rack. To my amazement I realized I was whistling. It hit me that I had turned a corner. I was okay. I would be okay from here on." He hadn't written anything that was publishable. But that wasn't the point. "What counted was that I had, after years of running from it, actually sat down and done my work. This was my epiphanal moment. My hero's journey was over. My artist's journey had begun."[2]

We encounter a similar narrative structure—despair that somehow gets turned to life and hope—all the time. Consider one of Christianity's most-told stories: the eucharistic narrative. Sometimes, when I receive Communion at church, I reflect on how the story of Jesus's life, death, and resurrection contains all elements of a complete narrative arc—problem, guide, hero, transformation, defeat, and surprising victory. But at its heart, it's also a story of bestowing. The story of Jesus's death and resurrection is bestowed in the eucharistic prayer, and the bread and wine are bestowed as a material token of Jesus's ongoing presence with us.[3]

Stories can help us celebrate life's joys—like the best toasts for a bride and groom at their rehearsal dinner. But they also guide us through our grimmest moments. The narrative patterns woven into every great story remind us that transformation often requires navigating difficulty (no Eucharist, after all, without crucifixion). This is especially true for writers, who must face their own all-is-lost moments while creating work that helps others through theirs.

What about those times when it seems like your writing life story is stuck or broken? When you're facing an immovable obstacle to the kind of life and writing practice you want, or you're in the middle of your current work-in-progress with zero ideas or time or energy necessary to move forward? Or you are convinced, again, that you're just not cut out to be a writer? What then? Start with receiving the gifts from story structure: consider despair as an ingredient in creating narrative tension, and be attentive to—no, search for!—the surprising life that might lurk on the other side of that despair.[4]

I reread portions of Steven Pressfield's *Nobody Wants to Read Your Shit* a dozen times during 2023, because, for many reasons, that was a year in which I needed to remember again and again that my all-is-lost moments aren't the end of the story. I needed consistent reminders that all-is-lost moments are always followed by epiphanal moments. Always.

On my second read-through, I underlined this passage. On read three, I highlighted it in pink.

> In the screenwriting trade, there's a concept called the All Is Lost moment. This moment usually comes about three-quarters of the way through the movie. It's the point in the story when the protagonist is farthest away from his or her goal.
>
> In the celluloid world, the All Is Lost moment is always followed by a breakthrough, a turnaround beat when despair becomes hope (or desperation that's the equivalent of hope) that propels the protagonist into action in Act Three.[5]

The film *Paterson* illustrates this beautifully. When Marvin destroys Paterson's notebook containing all his poems, we witness an all-is-lost moment that transforms into an opportunity for growth. This happens near the end of the film when Paterson, played by Adam Driver, and Laura break their routine to celebrate her cupcake earnings with a dinner and movie date.[6] After they return home and see the mess Marvin has made, the loss is devastating to Paterson, visible through "minute shifts in Driver's placid performance."[7] While he claims disinterest in publishing his poems, their destruction deeply affects him, as these poems represented his intimate observations and creative work. However, this moment transforms into an opportunity for growth. After losing his poems, Paterson meets a stranger on a bench who talks with him about poetry and gives him a new notebook. This interaction helps him begin again, suggesting that the creative process is more important than the finished product. The film shows how even apparent losses can lead to renewal, as every poem he has written before has prepared him to write additional poems moving forward. So, in a way, returning to what we know about how all of life is the writing life, the poems Marvin destroyed aren't lost forever. The process of writing those poems—and the poems themselves—formed Paterson to be who he will be when he decides to write again. In fact, his new poems wouldn't even exist if the previous ones hadn't existed and been destroyed first. What makes this all-is-lost moment a bit different than one you might find in films like *The Matrix* or *Star Wars* is how Paterson handles it. He stays calm and gracious. Unlike in typical film narratives, this crisis doesn't create conflict between characters or lead to dramatic confrontations. Instead, it demonstrates how loss can be met with acceptance and lead to new beginnings. How a gift from another writer can generate the gift of beginning again.

When a writer experiences despair, our very craft—what we know of the rhythms of narrative arcs—can restore our hope. Our craft teaches us that this part of the story, the feeling that the world is ending, is not in fact the end. More is coming. Sometimes you must move through the all-is-lost moment and enter the epiphanal moment before any alternatives or opportunities for growth appear.

My willingness to initially embrace the idea that all of life is the writing life emerged from an all-is-lost moment after my father died from COVID complications. Struggling with depression and complicated grief, I was too exhausted to write more than occasional social media posts. But not writing wasn't the solution—writing had always been how I processed life and discovered what I believed.

The epiphanal moment arrived when I realized my writerly identity wasn't something I could simply shed like a parka. I began to wonder: How could I reframe what it means to be a writer to hold space for my grief-filled reality? This led to a deeper understanding of the creative process—ideas don't only come at our laptops. We encounter countless details daily that will influence our future writing. If part of writing is passive and the process of becoming who we will be matters, perhaps all moments count.

Once I had this epiphany, hope returned. I knew the grief would eventually lift *because that's how stories work.*

My past narrative arcs reminded me I had healed before. The grief and depletion would form me into who I was becoming and who I'd need to be when I was ready to return to my writing practice. My anxiety about not writing didn't disappear, but it dissipated, allowing me to enter fully into what the present season required.

After letting my body weep and rest and weep and rest, I eventually had more energy to take notes. As my healing progressed, I wrote more often. And throughout that whole process, I learned one of the biggest lessons about creativity and making art I'd ever had the honor of learning. It might be *the* biggest lesson of my entire life because this idea applies to many areas, not just how to inhabit the writing life.

Wait for the epiphanies, for the story to unfold and show you what's next.

Bestow Through Intercessory Prayer

Writers often bestow their gifts through words on the page, but there's another powerful way we offer ourselves to others—through various forms of intercessory prayer. This kind of prayer emerges naturally from the writing life, as our creative work makes us more attuned to the universal experiences we all share. When we write about or navigate loneliness, grief, creative blocks, or spiritual questioning, we develop a special sensitivity to these struggles in others. We are more equipped to support others facing similar challenges. This awareness naturally flows into our prayer life, allowing us to stand in the gap for fellow writers with greater understanding and compassion.

After some spiritual direction sessions, I often find myself holding writers' struggles in prayer long beyond our meetings' end. Writers' questions about their identity and desires, their creative doubts and search for meaning—these concerns don't disappear when we end our Zoom calls. Instead, they become part of my own ongoing conversation with the divine, a way of bestowing care that extends past my scheduled time with directees.[1]

This practice of praying for other writers creates a hidden network of support within the literary community.

When a writer shares their work in a cowriting session, when someone voices their creative fears in a group gathering, when a colleague mentions their struggle with rejection—these moments become invitations to bestow prayer. Like the liturgical elements that structure our writing practice, intercessory prayer provides a framework for honoring others' needs before the divine.[2]

The act of praying for others often leads to concrete actions—sending an encouraging note, sharing a relevant poem, or providing an Uber Eats gift card. Prayer and practical care work together, each informing and deepening the other. This combination of spiritual and tangible assistance creates a more complete form of bestowing, one that addresses both seen and unseen need.

Having frequent conversations with writers has made me more in touch with difficulties they experience in all areas of life, shaping how I pray for both individuals and the broader writing community. When I notice themes emerging across multiple spiritual direction sessions or writing groups, these patterns often become part of my regular intercession—prayers for those feeling disconnected from their creativity, for writers struggling to trust their voice, for those seeking deeper belonging in their work.

One way to pray for others is to carry others' concerns into a prayer labyrinth. As Rhonda Mawhood Lee explains in her book *Seek and You Will Find*:

> The Christian labyrinth is an unbroken circular path leading to a central point and back out again. There's one path in and one path out, no blind alleys, no

> cunning builder to outwit. . . . You've probably seen a labyrinth somewhere. Churches build them outside, of bricks, stone, colored glass, even low hedges; sometimes they lay indoor labyrinths of tile; often, they purchase or create portable labyrinths painted on canvas that can be laid down for a retreat day or Lenten practice. You may also have seen a finger labyrinth: a flat disc embracing the labyrinth's circular shape, to be traced contemplatively when walking a labyrinth (or rolling in a wheelchair) isn't possible.[3]

Labyrinths offer a way to pray with our bodies, and the rhythmic movement of walking or tracing these ancient patterns can help quiet our minds and open our hearts to others' needs. If you live near a labyrinth, make a visit. If you don't live near one, you can print out labyrinth pages that can then be traced with your finger or a pencil. Or draw your own simple spiral on a plain piece of paper. Use your finger or a pen or pencil to follow the coiling path to the center. You can let the movement of your walking or tracing be the prayer while you hold a specific person or a broader writing community in the light of your soulful presence.

Here are additional instructions for a gentle walk in a prayer labyrinth:

1. Walk into the middle of the prayer labyrinth with both hands closed tight into fists and thinking about the worries others are holding.
2. When you get to the middle of the prayer labyrinth, open your hands and breathe and say a prayer if you

like, or just say out loud or whisper your intercessions, your wishes, for others.

3. As you leave the center of the prayer labyrinth, continue to meditate on the people or circumstances you carried with you into the labyrinth. Perhaps envision the names or faces of those for whom you pray.

The practice of intercessory prayer provides space for deeper connection within the writing community. It reminds us that our creative work exists within a web of relationships, both seen and unseen. Through intercessory prayer, we participate in a form of bestowing that transcends our immediate reach. While our words might touch those who read them, our prayers can support writers we've never met, uplift those working in solitude, and contribute to the larger creative ecosystem in ways we may never see but can trust are meaningful.

Bestow Through Grace

Embracing grace and its kindnesses can be a new way forward. I witnessed an example of a writer bestowing good things on others during a poetry workshop I attended a few years ago. And what I saw was a sort of care and consideration that made me want to be a kinder person.

Seconds after the facilitator shared his thoughts on the poem "What You Missed That Day You Were Absent from Fourth Grade" by Brad Aaron Modlin, a workshop participant several rows behind me raised her hand. When a moderator called on her, she began arguing that Modlin was doing something in the poem that the workshop leader had just made clear the poet was definitely not doing.

Annoyed, I lifted my eyebrows and glanced from side to side to see if anyone else seemed to think this woman was rude and oblivious, speaking up even though she clearly hadn't been listening. No one's eyes locked with mine to share a satisfying, knowing look of frustration, so I waited to see how the person up front would handle this situation. I doubted he would say anything along the lines of what I was thinking: "Did you listen to anything I said for the past ten minutes? This is not a literal list of lesson plans Modlin's fourth grade teacher taught when he was home sick or out of town for his grandmother's funeral. How could you even think that's what this poem is doing?"

Of course, he didn't say anything of the sort. Instead, he was kind to the woman who'd missed the point. He even managed to use her comment to spark a brief but enlightening conversation. The generous and compassionate response to her and a few others who chimed in during their back-and-forth was pretty much the opposite of the response my heart, mind, and soul wanted to deliver in that moment. He offered her grace and made her look smart. I was both chastened and mesmerized.

Few people I meet in the course of my daily grind actually inspire me to be kinder. Few people act in a way that spurs me to think "I want more of *that* in my life." The exchange over Modlin's poem was the first of several that unfolded similarly during our weeklong workshop nestled in the Hudson Valley, just past peak leaf season. The workshop leader's kindness was what struck me most in that gorgeous place with so many beautiful things to give my attention to, and his kindness is what I have carried with me most in the months and years since that trip.

I tend to ignore the importance of being kind because I've been inundated by toxic positivity, disingenuous politeness, and manipulative niceness my entire life as a Christian woman in the Deep South. Perhaps in my efforts to avoid such things, I've traveled too far to the other side of the spectrum. I can be harsh in the name of honesty. I can be mean in the name of frankness. But ever since I saw someone with authority and influence treat others with kindness during that autumn week in 2022,

I've become fonder of kindness and more aware of opportunities to show it to others. I still have plenty of room for improvement, but I believe it's safe to say I am a kinder person overall now than I was five years ago. The writing process has taught me kindness—the patient work of revision shows me how to give words and ideas second and third chances, how to look beneath surface flaws for hidden potential, how to stay with something difficult until understanding emerges. And I can't help but think that the poet's kindness, at least in part, has been formed by the poems he sits with and meditates on in ways that feel like a form of *lectio divina* with poetry.

So much of the writing life—indeed, so much of life—is dependent upon the giving and receiving of grace. The grace of the transforming power of words, of a deeper silence, of a calmer nervous system, of the depthless depth of God. The grace of bestowing good things on ourselves and others even if no one deserves it—even if there are plenty of perfectly reasonable objections and reasons to withhold.

While I claim that my Christian faith life is marked by a robust theology of grace, at times I feel its absence in my writing life. I want the writer who offended me on social media to be punished somehow. I want to withhold charity from best-selling authors of superficial fluff. At the same time, I want to feel free to post a biting comment without pushback, be anti-establishment without the establishment having opinions, and drop the ball and miss deadlines without suffering consequences for those actions. I want to receive goodness and grace when I do miss that deadline. But it's not grace if I'm the only recipient. It's not grace if it's dependent upon me receiving grace first or in return.

Learning to extend grace to others in the writing life begins with giving it to ourselves. When we practice receiving grace—accepting our imperfections, forgiving our missteps, embracing our humanity—we become more capable of bestowing it freely on others. This practice often becomes apparent in how we handle daily frustrations and perceived failures.

One way to be kind to ourselves and our nervous systems is to have a proper perspective regarding crises and noncrises. Ten years ago, I was more apt to respond to minor things as though they were crises, and now I'm much more capable of responding to a minor thing as one should respond to a minor thing and to the very few actual crises as one should respond to crises. In turn, my writing practice has changed because I'm able to ignore more of the distractions that used to pull me away from my writing.

For the past few years, I've refused to fall into crisis mode when circumstances don't merit a crisis response. Most of my false crises appear on the radar when I've failed to meet a definite or imagined deadline. Maybe I don't get to the post office in a timely manner because it always takes more effort than I think it should take to get to the post office in a timely manner. Perhaps I forget to do something I was supposed to do, something I want to do. My new next-door neighbor invites me to a Prosecco tasting and I forget to add it to my calendar so I forget to go and it feels like I've missed the single opportunity to establish a friendship with my might-have-been host. Some of my false crises begin when other people don't come through for me in some real or perceived manner. Maybe a workshop speaker is sick and can't be at an event I've organized. A friend is inattentive and ignoring my text messages. A child is home for the holidays and putting time with friends before time with me. False crises gain momentum when I imagine the worst possibilities and outcomes—my business is a sham, I should quit writing, I'm a terrible neighbor, the relationship is over, my kids hate me.

Practicing not falling into crisis reverses the cycle. I enter from the back door. First comes the mind, then the body. Instead of a storm of worst-case scenarios, I ask myself if the interruption, disruption, missed deadline, unmet expectations, change of plans, failed idea, or other occurrence is life-threatening. The answer is usually no. I pause and think through the current reality. I tell myself I'm safe, we're safe. Things aren't going as desired, but sandbags and plywood are unnecessary. Relax both shoulders. Release the jaw. Take six deep breaths with a six-count inhale and a six-count exhale.

False crises dissipate and turn from huge red rotating systems to green smatterings when I choose to imagine more realistic possibilities and outcomes. Businesses have all kinds of hiccups, and not mailing a candle at the earliest opportunity is not going to be the reason everything shuts down. Writers miss deadlines all the time because life happens. Friendships don't fail because of one misstep. My children's actions during Christmas break aren't determinative for the entirety of our relationships.

When my mind and body are assured, when I know that mandatory evacuation is not a requirement and my thoughts are more in line with reality, I ask God for creative solutions to obstacles. Then I make new plans, acknowledge and grieve losses, and replace the old narratives with new ones that account for the current circumstances.

Most days are full of reminders of what's not a crisis. Not getting my way is not a crisis. Not writing is not a crisis. Not having great engagement with what I think is a fantastic Instagram post is not a crisis. My unanswered emails, unending to-do list, dreams-in-progress, books-in-progress, life-in-progress—and don't forget these dirty floors and that pile of overdue library books. None of this is a crisis. At least not yet. But all is grace.

And when we clear out the false crises, we have more mental space for receiving and offering kindness and grace; we are more apt to receive and offer love. In a world full of hate fueled by fear and division, gifts of love can transform the giver and her recipient. With hearts tuned to love, we move toward broader belonging, we become fuller versions of who we were made to be, and we see opportunities to behold greater goodness.

Bestow from the Center

One gift I give myself and invite others to give themselves is a deeper soul silence that we access through cultivating a more contemplative way of writing and being present over time. My experiences with silence and solitude are much different than when I first began these faith and creativity practices twenty years ago. I have more access than I once did to an inner silence of mind, heart, and soul amid external chaos, angst, and difficulty, and so I can navigate all of life and writing from a more restful posture. This deeper silence isn't just for me and my own flourishing. It also takes me beyond myself and into more meaningful community with other people.

Martin S. Laird wrote this in *Into the Silent Land*:

> The more we journey towards the Center the closer we are both to God and to each other. The problem of feeling isolated from both God and others is overcome in the experience of the Center. This journey into God and the profound meeting of others in the inner ground of silence is a single movement. Exterior isolation is overcome in interior communion. . . . People who have gone fairly deeply into the contemplative path become open and vital people (however differently they may live this out). In this depthless depth we are caught up in a unity that grounds,

affirms, and embraces all diversity. Communion with God and communion with others are realizations of the same Center.[1]

Awareness of and sensitivity to the presence of the divine underlie my belief that all of life is the writing life. It's from this Center that we live and move and have our being. It's from this Center that we create and are shaped to make our art. What a gift! When I'm more connected to the Center, I write more regularly, and in turn I'm a fuller version of who I was created to be. I'm less affected by the inevitable distractions and interruptions and view them as necessary elements of the creative process. I'm kinder to myself and to others because I'm not grasping for power or influence or trying to manipulate others into coming through for me in ways that make me feel better about my life and my writing.

It's impossible to be fully centered every moment of every day. Daily life gives us too many opportunities to drift over to the periphery. When we feel disconnected from the Center, we can pause and determine how to reestablish a sense of connectedness. We can consider our recent and current belongings, becomings, and beholdings. We can check in with how we've been relating to time. We can read, write, walk, and pray. We can put ourselves in the way of art.

When we bestow from the Center, our gifts carry a different quality—one that flows from genuine desire rather than obligation. Our words emerge from a deeper well of compassion. We offer not just our creativity but the central core of our presence.

Bestow Through Action

Contemplation prepares us for action. When we have an enhanced sense of belonging and have put ourselves in the way of practices, rhythms, and rituals that help us become more of who we were made to be, we will be better prepared to behold with wonder various things that cross our paths. We will be quicker to bestow good things on ourselves and others. And we will be more able to act, in ways large and small, for the common good.

Rebecca Solnit tells a powerful story about how a single act of bestowing transformed her writing life. A friend gave her a Victorian writing desk—"a dainty piece of furniture" with "four narrow drawers" and "various kinds of ornamentation." This desk, which Solnit still uses today, has carried "millions of words: more than twenty books, reviews, essays, love letters," and countless emails. But the story of how she received it reveals the profound impact of bestowing. A year before giving Solnit the desk, this friend had survived a horrific assault by an ex-boyfriend who tried to silence her. The friend had received the desk as payment from a single mother who was being evicted and then passed it on to Solnit. "Someone tried to silence her," Solnit writes. "Then she gave me a platform for my voice." This act of bestowing became foundation for all of Solnit's future work—literally and metaphorically.[1]

Sometimes our bestowing flows from creative abundance and a strong literary spirit, like Kaveh Akbar's free monthly Zoom gatherings[2] and Jami Attenberg's rallying writers to write one thousand words a day for two weeks, providing inspiration and encouragement through daily emails to all who participate.[3] But our actions don't need to be connected to writing. They can be small, ordinary displays of charity. Volunteer for a local arts nonprofit. Take your nephew to the zoo. Skip takeout for two weeks and donate the money saved to the Red Cross. Read books to kindergarteners at your neighborhood's elementary school.

In the grand scheme of things, our writing is not all about us. It's about being a part of something bigger, contributing what we can to the common good, entering conversations that have been taking place for hundreds and thousands of years, and knowing that the words we write will benefit readers directly and people in our immediate circles indirectly. What actions will help you know you are a part of something larger than yourself? What will benefit your full self *and* the greater common good? Your actions toward these ends may need to be more contemplative for now. Maybe you need to take a nap, or take a quiet walk, or undertake some other action that will help you embrace different actions tomorrow or next week. Or, perhaps this week, or this day, is when you have the space and the desire to act more directly for the good of your surrounding community: bake a casserole for your local church's breakfast ministry; take your friend's three kids to the park so that she can finish her sonnet; write your congressperson.

Every act of bestowing contains elements of giving and receiving that create possibility for what comes next. If you aren't sure what actions you want to take, enter the cycle through contemplation. And just as contemplation prepares us for action, action points us toward more contemplation. If you are coming out of a season of intense work or writing, perhaps you need a long stretch of rest and remembering. Return to the examen practice described in an earlier chapter and take a few minutes to review the past week or so. Check in with where you are right now. Which turn of the cycle are you winding around? Don't force anything. Let the process unfold naturally as you notice what's stirring in your gut, head, and heart. Trust that each small act of bestowing through words, presence, or practical support contributes to the spiral of creativity and connection that sustains us all.

Begin Again

The beginning is always today.

—Mary Shelley

To begin again is to participate in a dance of renewal, where ending and beginning blur together like dusk and dawn. We return to the poem we started writing last week, the journals we haven't opened in several days, or the creative communities we haven't seen in months, not because we failed yesterday but because the spiral of creativity calls us back, inviting us to discover what this "again" might reveal.

When you begin again, you have an opportunity to trust the spiral nature of creativity, where each return carries forward what you've already learned while opening to fresh possibility. Like the holiday seasons of Advent and Christmas, of Lent and Easter, that cycle through familiar patterns and traditions yet never replicate, every "again" holds both memory and possibility, both knowing and not knowing.

Writers are always beginning again. With each new draft, each additional writing session, each return to a familiar theme, we spiral into more astute understanding. The word "again" comes from "ongean," meaning "toward, against, in return."[1] *The suggestion of movement pushes both forward and back, like waves approaching and retreating from the shore or breath moving in and out of the body.*

In spiritual direction, we learn that "again" isn't about perfect repetition but about faithful return. We come back to the page after rejection, to the practice after interruption, to the work after rest. Each return transforms both the writer and the writing. The person who begins again today brings new wisdom, new questions, new possibilities to the work.

In the last stanza of the final poem of Four Quartets, *T. S. Eliot wrote:*

> *We shall not cease from exploration*
> *And the end of all our exploring*
> *Will be to arrive where we started*
> *And know the place for the first time.*[2]

This is the gift of beginning again—finding new depths in familiar territory, discovering fresh insight in old stories while meeting yourself anew in the recurring rhythms of creative practice.

Beginning again interweaves all the essential practices of a writer's spiritual journey. We belong to communities that welcome our returns, understanding that creative rhythms include both presence and absence. Through repeated practice, we become more fully ourselves as writers, each "again" adding another layer to our voice and insights. When we begin once more, we behold our work with fresh eyes, discovering nuances we missed before and seeing familiar territory from a different perspective. And even in starting over, we bestow our gifts—offering our attention, sharing our struggles, and contributing to the ongoing conversations. We discover that beginning again isn't a setback but a spiral deeper into the creative process.

Begin Again Through Returning

Sarah is crying in her guest room. While she is stretched out, lying on her back on the hardwood floor of her home in Morgantown, West Virginia, I'm sitting on top of the bed. My view of her is from up above. I'm an audience member at a play with a decent seat and clear line of sight of the entire stage. A small lamp on the nightstand provides our only light, but the visibility is clear enough to see my friend who has needed a big cry for the past three days. I want to move toward her and offer a hug or place my hand on her shoulder. I want to give her some sort of physical touch offering, but part of what's exhausted her to the point of tears is too many people requiring a response of her. Right now, no child needs her mind, body, or words, so I stay where I am and give her as much time and space as she needs to let everything out without worrying about anything else. I wish she were an actor in a play that only has one act left, with plans for a festive after-party and a few days off before the next show. But this is reality. There's no costume to hang up. No break from the part she is playing as an exhausted mom of two young kids.

Sarah's eyes and body have been telling me she's depleted since I arrived to help take care of the two boys, ages six months and two years, while her husband was out of town. Even though Sarah is fifteen years younger than me, our friendship is easy. I was thrilled to plan my first trip to her home, have some time to catch up in person, and assist in the care of her children. Our conversations usually include talk of what we're reading and writing, what everyone else is reading and writing, what we hope to read and write. I was looking forward to babysitting and giving her time each day to leave the house and disappear into a coffee shop or bookstore. But it became very clear very quickly that Sarah would not be going anywhere. Instead of asking her about essays and book chapters, research and reading lists, I've been peppering her with questions about basic human needs. "When was the last time you drank water? What about protein? Want to nap while I watch Thomas the Tank Engine videos with the kids?" The kids were fine: well fed, clean, happy. But Sarah was malnourished in every possible way, including losing the habit of reading or writing.

When I haven't written for several days or weeks because of illness or travels or other interruptions, I know what to do when it's time to jump back in. I return to what I aspire to do most days: I read, write, walk, pray, and see some art. These are the five basic rhythms that help me inhabit the writing life I want and need. Right now, I'm in the early stages of a new project and I'm still getting that mildly overwhelmed feeling I sometimes get with untrodden beginnings. When those feelings arise, I know I need to read, write, walk, pray, and encounter art.

The rhythms, rituals, cycles, and spirals of the writing life are always waiting for us to return to them. You may have established a meaningful daily or weekly ritual—the weekly reading of a short story, the nightly writing of a haiku—but then you skip it for two days or two weeks or months: you can always start again. It's fine. Really. If anything you've established as a sustainable writing practice begins to feel like a rule that is too restrictive or no longer serves your writing goals, maybe stop for a while and try something new. Or at least pause long enough to ask yourself why it feels restrictive. Rituals and cycles should provide a restful and comfortable welcome to greater nurture and freedom. Belonging, becoming, beholding, and bestowing should be viewed as gentle invitations to begin again.

When it's time for the writing that began in the dark to find its way through the light, make a cup of tea and take it to your desk alongside that sparkling water or glass of juice. (Most writers prefer multiple beverages while writing, right?)

What's the problem you face when you sit down? You want to write, but obstacles multiply like rabbits. Time evaporates. Your will vanishes precisely when you have a free hour. You long to write when life is chaos, then resist when quiet finally arrives. You tell yourself everything must be perfect—the house clean; the planets aligned (but not Mercury in retrograde); the laundry folded; family, pets, or friends content. As if writing requires an impossible arrangement of circumstances rather than simply showing up to bestow your gifts.

The deeper problem isn't just finding time or perfect conditions. It's facing the void of uncertainty. No one will make us write. No one will guarantee that our words matter. The darkness holds all our questions: What if it's all wasted effort? What if I should just quit? What if I deleted all traces of this dream and filled my life with easier pursuits—more reading, longer walks, anything but this vulnerable act of creating?

But here's what we know: The creative life we explored through belonging, becoming, and beholding prepared us for this moment of beginning again and bestowing our gifts, even in darkness. We keep writing because something in us must. Each return to the page becomes both offering and invitation, a way of saying yes to what's waiting to emerge this time we sit down and do the work.

When I was with Sarah during the visit described above, she was barely getting by. It was not the time to suggest she experiment with nourishing rhythms that might move her closer to the writing life she wants. But I did suggest she do what she could to *return to herself.* After my visit, she decided to take a few weeks off from her part-time job to catch up on sleep and allocate additional time and energy to the current demands of parenting. She and her husband began creating healthier individual and family routines. She got so much better. And she began writing again. We even met up halfway between our homes for a four-day writing retreat that autumn after the tearful summer evening on the floor of her guest room.

Begin Again with Abundance and Seasons

When we understand that beginning again is part of nature's abundance, we can approach our writing rhythms with greater gentleness and trust. As spring follows winter with its generous display of blooms, or as fallen leaves nourish soil for future growth, our creative practice operates in cycles of fullness and fallow times.

One of the Scripture verses that was central to my childhood in the church is John 10:10, in which Jesus says, "I am come that they might have life, and that they might have it more abundantly" (KJV). But abundance isn't just about constant happiness or comfort—it's about experiencing the full spectrum of life. If Jesus came so we could have life abundantly, he came so we could have an abundance of all things—the ups and downs, rest and struggle, sorrow and joy, tragedy and celebration. An abundant life includes having a thriving marriage while knowing the heartache of broken relationships. It's enjoying meaningful work and experiencing seasons of depletion. It's tasting God's presence and facing spiritual loneliness.

Abundance weaves through every aspect of our writing life when we remain open to its presence. In belonging, it appears as the endless capacity of writing communities to welcome one more voice and additional perspectives. In becoming, it emerges as the infinite possibilities for growth every time we approach the page with each draft revealing extra layers of insight and awareness. In beholding, abundance shows up as the inexhaustible invitation to see familiar things anew—how the same tree outside our window offers different gifts in morning light, afternoon shadow, and evening dusk. And in bestowing, abundance flows through the countless ways our words can transform us and touch others. Creative abundance flows in cycles of giving and receiving, growth and rest. We can honor these natural rhythms by paying attention to the world around us—how seasons unfold in predictable yet surprising ways, how nature demonstrates the perfect timing of dormancy and bloom.

I learned about the cycles and seasons specific to my hometown from an unexpected source: the previous owner of our first house. When Tim and I became the second owners of our first house in Homewood in November 1998, we inherited Thelma's magnificent spring yard. That first February and March revealed nature's careful choreography: First came dozens of daffodils, their lemon-colored petals fanning around trumpets across the side yard and above the ivy-covered retaining wall. Next, the lone forsythia bush blazed yellow-gold in the front yard. Then the Bradford pear trees across the street unfurled their snowy white blooms, perfectly framed by our living room window. The finale arrived with the tulip tree's dark purple ovals and the ornamental cherry trees' delicate pink blossoms.

Like Thelma's carefully orchestrated garden, the

writing life follows its own seasonal rhythms. Writers throughout time have recognized these natural cycles in their work. Audre Lorde used spring's renewal to process political upheaval in "Second Spring," while Alice Walker found creative restoration in her garden's seasonal rhythms. Toni Morrison discovered inspiration in the communal cycles of her writing group's monthly gatherings, while Camille Dungy structured her groundbreaking anthology *Black Nature* around ten natural cycles that shape how we experience the earth. Like the landscapes they wrote about, these writers understood how creativity moves through patterns of dormancy and abundance.

Nature teaches us that cycles are not merely repetitive but transformative. Each season carries forward the wisdom of those who came before while creating conditions for what lies ahead. Just as soil needs both rain and sunshine, writers need periods of gathering and releasing, of input and output. Understanding these cycles helps us trust the process when words flow easily and when they seem distant.

It makes sense that writing would be easier for me in spring because most things are easier during this time of year. Basketball season is over, so I'm not busy watching and discussing my son's games. The warmer, brighter weather boosts my mood. The days are longer. Last week Tim told me the sun wouldn't set before six o'clock again until October. "We made it," he said victoriously. Spring brings renewed energy to both garden and page. The words flow more easily in this season, with fewer obstacles between mind and page. Summer becomes more challenging—a season of fits and starts, like a garden requiring constant attention. Winter is hit or miss, and I've learned to honor December's fallow period.

Now, in our seventh house, my young forsythia plants remind me that spring's cycles continue. Thank God the forsythia returns each year. Like the forsythia's reliable return, writing finds its rhythm in nature's patterns. Each bloom represents the possibility of beginning again, of finding fresh words in familiar seasons. The key isn't forcing ourselves to write in every season, but recognizing how each season offers its own invitation to creativity—whether it's spring's burst of energy, summer's languid afternoons, autumn's reflective mood, or winter's quiet contemplation.

Begin Again with Nourishing Rhythms

Nourishing rhythms anchor us through life's cycles of creativity and loss. Like familiar constellations guiding ancient sailors, these practices help us navigate both calm seas and stormy waters. Whether we're experiencing creative abundance or drought, personal celebration or grief, our rhythms provide touchstones for beginning again.

Sometimes beginning again means returning to the most basic elements of our practice—picking up a pen, taking a deep breath. Other times it means honoring the fallow periods, trusting that rest and reflection are as essential to creativity as active production. The key is recognizing that each return to our rhythms deepens our relationship with both the practice and our writerly selves.

Writers throughout history have relied on personal rhythms to sustain their creative lives. Janet Frame's silence became a necessity for her writing. Mary Oliver's morning walks birthed countless poems.[1] Virginia Woolf insisted on writing frequent diary entries to feed her imagination.[2] These weren't just habits but sacred rhythms that created space for both inspiration and healing.

When life interrupts our writing practice—through loss, illness, major life changes, or simple daily demands—our established rhythms offer the route back to ourselves and our work. They remind us that creativity, like nature, moves in cycles of activity and rest, gathering and release.

On the first Tuesday of August 2020, when I suspected my dad was dying, I claimed the living room sofa as my grief station. For four days, I slept and woke and slept again, only moving for essential needs. By the fifth day, I knew the only way to counter the effects of being on the sofa for so long was to no longer be on the sofa. This, too, was a kind of beginning again—the first tentative steps back into the world of the living.

One reason my dad died was his long battle with type 2 diabetes. When COVID-19 struck, his body couldn't fight it. Three years before his death, I was diagnosed with mild insulin resistance. Walking most days is the best thing I can do for my health. It's also one of my nourishing rhythms that helps me have the writing life I want. So that Saturday evening, two days after his death, I texted my friend Kelly: "I need to go for a walk. Make sure Tim and I go." In asking for help, I was choosing to begin again.

Tim and I walked down Manhattan Street—a straight shot that required few decisions. Behind my sunglasses, I cried while Tim walked beside me in his own grief. The sidewalks and asphalt asked me to keep putting one foot in front of the other—each step a small act of beginning again. After returning home, I slid under my favorite heirloom quilt on the sofa and took notes on my phone. I wanted to remember how walking made me want to write. Even though I didn't have the energy to write what I wanted to write, I had the energy to make it possible to write about this another day.

If you haven't written in a while, or if you aren't sure if you're a "real writer" (you are!), you can begin writing again or for the first time today. Right now. You can find a pencil and paper and write a word or phrase or sentence. Then you can do it again and again. You can begin again any day, any morning, any evening. Even now.

Begin Again and Again

When you need to begin again with your writing practice—whether after a long illness, a bout of creative resistance, a big life change like a move or new job, or inevitable ordinary interruptions—you can enter through any point in the cycle of belonging, becoming, beholding, and bestowing. Like a spiral staircase that allows access at multiple levels, each element offers a unique doorway back to the page.

Perhaps you'll begin again through belonging—by joining a writing group or attending a reading. Maybe you'll return through becoming—by allowing yourself to be formed by whatever season you're in, trusting that even apparent setbacks are shaping who you'll be when you write again. Beholding might draw you back through paying attention to the ordinary moments of your days, letting curiosity guide you toward fresh insights. Or bestowing could be your entry point by sharing a small piece of writing with a friend or simply showing up to the page as an act of generosity toward yourself. As you behold the world with greater attention, you have more to bestow. When you bestow your gifts, you discover new ways of belonging and becoming. Through belonging, we find the communities and connections that support our returns.

Each time we begin again, we're reminded that we don't write alone—we're part of generations of writers who have wrestled with words before us. In becoming, we recognize that everything we encounter shapes who we are as writers. Every draft, every return to the notebook after absence transforms us. Beholding teaches us that each beginning offers fresh eyes. What we couldn't see yesterday might reveal itself today. And through bestowing, we learn that every beginning is also a gift—to ourselves, to our readers, to the larger conversation our words join. Even in starting over, we offer something valuable: our presence, our persistence, our willingness to engage with mystery.

Trust that all of life is the writing life, and that every experience has been forming you for this new beginning. Some days we'll write pages; others we'll barely manage a sentence. Some seasons will overflow with creativity; others will require patient tending of fallow ground. This too is abundance—the fullness of a life lived in conversation with words and spirit.

Remember that beginning again isn't failure but faithfulness. Each return to the page is a declaration that your voice matters, your stories matter, your presence matters, you matter. The spiral always invites us deeper, and the invitation remains open.

Let's do what we do. Let's begin again.

Acknowledgments

I am deeply grateful to the entire Eerdmans team—especially to Lisa Ann Cockrel, whose guidance and expertise helped this book become what it was always meant to be.

To the Spiritual Direction for Writers® community: thank you for your presence, for reminding me that I am not alone in this writing life. This book is yours as much as it is mine.

Lauren Winner generously offered support and insight at critical moments.

Erin Griffin Collum and Riley Donlon read early drafts and devoted countless hours to my sources and endnotes—a true act of love.

Others read chapters, discussed ideas, provided feedback, and encouraged me to keep going. Heartfelt thanks especially to my mother, Cathy Byrd, also to Bettina Byrd-Giles, Tanya Davis, Michael Dechane, Kelly Denson, Anna Gazmarian, Liz Charlotte Grant, Marlena Graves, Elisa Muñoz-Miller, Sarah Orner, Allen Proctor, Regan Rose Read, Catherine Ricketts, Rachel Sheild, Stacy Siegel, Mary Bea Sullivan, and Carla Jean Whitley.

Thanks to the Collegeville Institute for time and space to write, and to my cohort for their gracious advice and recommendations as I shaped this book's earliest pages.

Communities like the Glen Workshop, Wild Goose Festival, and Alabama Writers Cooperative gave me places to share and refine these ideas.

Thank you to Cal and Sri at Church Street Coffee & Books for creative encouragement and endless coffee; to Magic Mind for fueling my focus; to Switchyards for aesthetically pleasing and writer-friendly coworking spaces; and to art museums, libraries, and bookstores everywhere for research, respite, and enabling my endless book habit.

The writing life can be solitary, but I am surrounded by communities who care immensely about both words and the soul: dear friends from the Birmingham poetry community, my MFA program, and the Glen Workshop have blessed me along the way.

Endless gratitude to my family for unwavering support: to my mother and grandmother—my greatest champions; to my cousin Hillary Hudson, for friendship, photography, and every last-minute design request; and to the many relatives and friends whose love shapes all my work.

To my children, Riley and Brady—your creativity and humor are my greatest delights, and you make me want to be a better writer.

To Tim, for your daily love and grace; for seeing both me and my work; for viewing my writing and spiritual direction vocations as vital contributions to something larger; and for bringing me coffee in bed.

Finally, I give thanks to God. I am more of who I was created to be when I am writing and accompanying others on their spiritual journeys.

Notes

A Prefatory Note

1. James Martin, *Learning to Pray: A Guide for Everyone* (HarperOne, 2022), 305. "Directee" is a term some people use for someone who receives spiritual direction from a spiritual director.

Pause with Toni Morrison

1. Pam Houston, "Toni Morrison: The Precious Moments a Writer Lives For," Oprah.com., July 2009, https://tinyurl.com/msx2wjnk.

2. "Toni Morrison Describes How She Began to Be a Writer," MacDowell, August 15, 2016, https://tinyurl.com/2kmhhdc4.

3. Toni Morrison, "A Conversation Between Toni Morrison and Frank McCourt," moderated by Juan Williams and the Connecticut Forum, May 4, 2001, YouTube, https://tinyurl.com/4kuxpde6.

4. Toni Morrison, "The Work You Do, the Person You Are," *New Yorker*, May 29, 2017, https://tinyurl.com/5ejj79p5.

Belong, Become, Behold, Bestow

1. Timothy Greenfield-Sanders, dir., *Toni Morrison: The Pieces I Am* (Magnolia Pictures, 2019).

2. Rebecca Solnit, *Recollections of My Nonexistence: A Memoir* (Viking, 2020), 47.

Begin

1. For more information on morning pages, see Julia Cameron, *The Artist's Way* (Tarcher, 2002).

Begin Where You Are

1. Dante Alighieri, *The Divine Comedy: Inferno*, trans. John Ciardi (Modern Library, 1996), 1–2.

2. Jesmyn Ward, *Let Us Descend* (Scribner, 2023), 1–2.

Begin with a New Perspective

1. Maryemma Graham, ed., *Conversations with Margaret Walker* (University Press of Mississippi, 2002), 59.

2. Matt Richtel, *Inspired: Understanding Creativity* (HarperCollins, 2022), 203.

Begin with Fifteen Minutes

1. Salaam Green, "Writing to Heal: Healing Through Poetry with Salaam Green," moderated by Hoover Public Library during Magic City Poetry Festival, May 3, 2021, YouTube, 1:27:34, https://tinyurl.com/yc6c2uyu.

Begin with Rest

1. Tricia Hersey, *Rest Is Resistance: Free Yourself from Grind Culture and Reclaim Your Life* (Aster, 2024), 6.

Begin with Your Breath

1. James Nestor, *Breath: The New Science of a Lost Art* (Riverhead Books, 2020), 83.

Begin with Prayer

1. Simone Weil, "Reflections on the Right Use of School Studies with a View to the Love of God," in *Waiting for God* (Routledge Classics, 1951), 61.

2. Frank Capra, dir., *It's a Wonderful Life* (Paramount, 1946).

3. Jason Mott, *Hell of a Book* (Dutton, 2021), 314.

4. Victoria Chang, *Dear Memory: Letters on Writing, Silence, and Grief* (Milkweed Editions, 2021), 85.

5. Weil, "Reflections on the Right Use," 67.

Begin with Rituals

1. Nicholas Hobson et al., "The Psychology of Rituals: An Integrative Review and Process-Based Framework," *Personality and Social Psychology Review* 22, no. 3 (2018): 260–84.

2. Hanif Abdurraqib (@nifmuhammad), "The Year In Flowers was also one of adapting and transforming rituals," Instagram, December 26, 2024, https://tinyurl.com/2rx3az58.

Begin with Cycles and Spirals

1. Hayley Verdi, "Seasonal Cycles and the Emotions of Faith in Christina Rossetti's *Goblin Market and Other Poems* (1862)," *Renascence* 76, no. 4 (2024): 242–61, 282.

2. Christina Rossetti, *Poems and Prose*, Oxford World's Classics (Oxford University Press, 2008), 56. Poem is in the public domain.

Belong to God

1. Brian Doyle, *Wet Engine: Exploring the Mad Wild Miracle of the Heart* (OSU Press, 2012), 6.

2. Art Lit with Thank You Books: Imani Perry and André Holland, public event at the Birmingham Museum of Art, February 9, 2025.

3. Imani Perry, *Black in Blues: How a Color Tells the Story of My People* (Ecco, 2025), 1.

4. Perry, *Black in Blues*, 3, 54, 86–89.

5. Melissa Febos, *Body Work: The Radical Power of Personal Narrative* (Catapult, 2022), 154.

Belong to Your Body

1. Tricia Hersey, *Rest Is Resistance: Free Yourself from Grind Culture and Reclaim Your Life* (Aster, 2024), 38.

2. Hersey, *Rest Is Resistance*, 38.

3. Aundi Kolber, *Strong like Water* (Tyndale Refresh, 2023), 147–48.

Belong to Time

1. Thomas Merton, *New Seeds of Contemplation* (New Directions, 2007), 9.

2. Martha Dickinson Bianchi, *Emily Dickinson Face to Face* (Houghton Mifflin, 1932), 60–66; Virginia Woolf, *A Room of One's Own* (Hogarth, 1929); "Toni Morrison: The Art of Fiction No. 134," interviewed by Elissa Schappell and Claudia Brodsky Lacour, *Paris Review*, no. 128 (Fall 1993), https://tinyurl.com/4yn9xecz.

Belong to the Liturgical Year

1. Micheal Hickerson, "Bobby Gross: Living the Christian Year," *Emerging Scholars Blog*, November 23, 2009, https://tinyurl.com/3839pucc.

Belong to a Literary Community

1. "Lifestyle and Legacy of the Bloomsbury Group," Tate Museum, accessed October 3, 2025, https://tinyurl.com/45rww6mc.

2. Vanessa Thorpe, "Discovered: A Lost Possible Inspiration for Virginia Woolf's Mrs Dalloway," *Guardian*, October 5, 2024, https://tinyurl.com/3wuvsw2j.

3. Maryemma Graham, *The House Where My Soul Lives: The Life of Margaret Walker* (Oxford University Press, 2022), 131.

4. From an email exchange with Dr. Robert Luckett on February 10, 2025.

5. Nefertiti Robinson and Danté Stewart, interview during a private online event facilitated by Charlotte Donlon, "Our Faith in Writing: Conversations on Art, Faith, Doubt, and Mystery," September 22, 2022.

Belong to Traditions

1. Scott Cairns, *Correspondence with My Greeks* (Slant Books, 2024), 9.

2. "Of Origins and Precursors: Q&A with Scott Cairns," Slant Books, August 22, 2024, https://tinyurl.com/2p4hxkn7.

3. Julian Murphet, "A Cosmic Ocean of Shame: Jesmyn

Ward's Let Us Descend Confronts a History Beyond the Ken of Storytelling," *Conversation*, November 5, 2023, https://tinyurl.com/hfmh6y2k.

4. Julia Kastner, "Maximum Shelf: Let Us Descend," *Shelf Awareness*, May 17, 2023, https://tinyurl.com/yc58mm7x.

5. Zoe Perzo, "A Q&A with Jesmyn Ward, Author of November Indie Next Top Pick 'Let Us Descend,'" American Booksellers Association, October 25, 2023, https://tinyurl.com/hvyy4ejb.

Belong to a Poem

1. Charlotte Donlon, host, *Our Faith in Writing*, podcast, episode 12, "Kaveh Akbar & Ashley M. Jones on Pilgrim Bell and Belonging Through Poetry Part Two," September 11, 2021, https://tinyurl.com/y7fmuz9t.

2. Ashley M. Jones, "God Made My Whole Body," in *Reparations Now!* (Hub City Press, 2021), 29. Used with permission. Reprinted from *Reparations Now!* Copyright 2021 by Ashley M. Jones. Used with permission of the publisher, Hub City Press. All rights reserved.

3. Kaveh Akbar, "How Prayer Works," in *Pilgrim Bell: Poems* (Graywolf, 2021), 55. From *Pilgrim Bell* by Kaveh Akbar published by Chatto & Windus. Copyright Kaveh Akbar, 2021. Reprinted by permission of The Random House Group Limited and The Permissions Company, LLC on behalf of Graywolf Press, graywolfpress.org.

Become Friends with Time

1. Kathleen Norris, *The Cloister Walk* (Riverhead Books, 1997), 6.

2. "About Monastic Prayer," Saint Bede Abbey, accessed October 3, 2025, https://tinyurl.com/3tuuxttd.

3. "Time Perception: Where Does Time Go?" Better Help, updated August 6, 2025, https://tinyurl.com/yc88fp3j.

4. "Time Perception and How Long Things Actually Take," Jo Van Every, April 1, 2020, https://tinyurl.com/28p97jzy.

5. Octavia E. Butler, *Kindred*, 25th ed. (Beacon, 2003).

6. Marcel Proust, *Swann's Way: In Search of Lost Time*, vol. 1, reprint ed. (Penguin Classics, 2004).

7. Virginia Woolf, *Mrs. Dalloway* (Penguin Classics, 2019).

8. Joy Harjo, "Perhaps the World Ends Here," in *The Woman Who Fell from the Sky: Poems* (Norton, 1996), 88.

9. Stacey Balkun, "The World Begins at a Kitchen Table," University of Arizona Poetry Center, July 30, 2019, https://tinyurl.com/bjy2bzvc.

10. Norris, *The Cloister Walk*, 43.

11. Saint Benedict Abbot of Monte Cassino, The Rule of St. Benedict in English, p. 29.

Become Familiar with Openings and Closings

1. Timothy M. Gallagher, *The Discernment of Spirits: An Ignatian Guide for Everyday Living* (Crossroad, 2005), 60, Kindle edition.

Become More at Peace with Uncertainty

1. John Kay and Mervyn King, *Radical Uncertainty: Decision-Making Beyond the Numbers* (Norton, 2020), 421–31.

2. Meghan O'Rourke, "I Teach Creative Writing. This Is What A.I. Is Doing to Students," *New York Times Magazine*, July 2025, https://tinyurl.com/23ac99xe.

3. Kay and King, *Radical Uncertainty*, 432–33.

Become Comfortable Asking More Questions

1. Quoting the exhibition here.

2. Toni Morrison, "Nobel Prize Lecture," The Nobel Prize, December 7, 1993, https://tinyurl.com/ypw7s6rv.

Become Even More Curious

1. Susan Scott Parrish, *American Curiosity: Cultures of Natural History in the Colonial British Atlantic World* (University of North Carolina Press, 2006), 189–90.

2. Ian Leslie, *Curious: The Desire to Know and Why Your Future Depends on It* (Basic Books, 2015), 19.

3. John Cage, *Silence: Lectures and Writings*, 50th anniversary ed. (Wesleyan University Press, 2012), 93.

Become a Writer Who Pauses

1. Adam Zagajewski, "Transformation," trans. Clare Cavanagh, in *Without End: New and Selected Poems* (Farrar, Straus & Giroux, 2002), 214.

Become a Writer Who Sits Alone in Silence

1. Timothy D. Wilson et al., "Just Think: The Challenges of the Disengaged Mind," *Science* 345 (2014): 75–77.

2. Janet Frame, *An Angel at My Table* (Women's Press, 2001), 356.

3. Frame, *An Angel at My Table*, 354–57.

4. Elaine Smookler, "The Power of Solitude," Mindful, July 26, 2017, https://tinyurl.com/mu4uh56y.

Become Someone Who Writes in the Dark

1. Ismar Schorsch, "The Day Begins with Night," Jewish Theological Seminary, October 25, 1997, https://tinyurl.com/47zs5c87.

Become a Little Neurotic

1. *The Collected Works of Saint Teresa of Avila*, vol. 1, trans. Kieran Kavanagh and Otilio Rodriguez (ICS Publications, 1987), 364.

Become Through Liturgy

1. *The Book of Common Prayer* (Church Publishing, 1979).

2. Edna St. Vincent Millay, "What Lips My Lips Have Kissed, and Where, and Why," in *Collected Poems* (Harper & Brothers, 1956), 602.

3. Eugene Peterson, *Eat This Book: A Conversation in the Art of Spiritual Reading* (Eerdmans, 2009), 74.

Behold

1. Mary Oliver, "The Summer Day," in *New and Selected Poems* (Beacon, 1992), 94; *The Gospel in Gerard Manley Hopkins: Selections from His Poems, Letters, Journals, and Spiritual Writings*, The Gospel in Great Writers (Plough, 2017), 58.

Behold Through Contemplation

1. Thomas Merton, *The Inner Experience: Notes on Contemplation* (HarperOne, 2012), 59.

2. Sophfronia Scott, *The Seeker and the Monk: Everyday Conversations with Thomas Merton* (Broadleaf Books, 2021), 14.

3. Scott, *The Seeker and the Monk*, 110.

4. Lauren F. Winner, *Wearing God: Clothing, Laughter, Fire, and Other Overlooked Ways of Meeting God* (HarperOne, 2015), 224–25.

Behold Through the Examen

1. Rhonda Mawhood Lee, *Seek and You Will Find: Discovering a Practice of Prayer* (Forward Movement, 2021), 112–13.

2. Diane V. Tomkinson, "Angela Foligno's Spiral Pattern of Prayer," in *Franciscans at Prayer*, ed. Timothy J. Johnson, The Medieval Franciscans, vol. 4 (Brill Academic, 2007), 195–219.

Behold with Your Body

1. John 20:24–29 KJV.

2. *Theological Dictionary of the New Testament*, ed. Gerhard Friedrich, trans. Geoffrey W. Bromiley, vol. 5 (Eerdmans, 1967), 325.

Behold the Ordinary

1. Jim Jarmusch, dir., *Paterson* (Amazon Studios, 2016).

2. Kathleen Norris and Gareth Higgins, *A Whole Life in Twelve Movies: A Cinematic Journey to a Deeper Spirituality* (Brazos, 2024), 55–56.

3. Stine Fantoft Berg, "Behind the Scenes: Ordinary Magazine," *Stack*, July 2016, https://tinyurl.com/mr369kb3.

4. Kathleen Norris, *The Quotidian Mysteries: Laundry, Liturgy, and "Women's Work"* (Paulist, 1998).

5. Norris, *The Quotidian Mysteries*, 12.

6. Mary Oliver, *New and Selected Poems*, vol. 1 (Beacon, 2013). Several of Oliver's poems from *New and Selected Poems*, vol. 1, help me connect more with this real, present, available world. A few on my list include "When Death Comes," "Little Owl Who Lives in the Orchard," "Gannets," "Whelks," and "Alligator Poem."

7. Norris, *The Quotidian Mysteries*, 10–11.

Behold Art

1. William M. Perthes, "Art, Well-Being, and Medicine at the Barnes Foundation," *Journal of Humanities in Rehabilitation*, accessed October 6, 2025, https://tinyurl.com/2sn89szm.

2. Alice Lok Cahana, "Miracles in Auschwitz: Word and Art as Kaddish," in *History (1933–1948): What We Choose to Remember*, ed. Margaret Monahan Hogan and James M. Lies (University of Portland, 2011), 35.

Behold the Outdoors

1. Margaret R. Ellsberg, "Incompatible Excellences," in *The Gospel in Gerard Manley Hopkins: Selections from His Poems, Letters, Journals, and Spiritual Writings*, by Gerard Manley Hopkins, The Gospel in Great Writers (Plough, 2017), 19.

2. Hopkins, *The Gospel in Gerard Manley Hopkins*, 58.

3. "Daily Nourishment for February 21, 2024: Hidden Silence with Hallie Waugh, Quieting Yourself, Music, and More," Spiritual Direction for Writers, February 21, 2024, https://tinyurl.com/5x9c73nk.

4. Learn more about Holly Carlisle and her work at https://www.hollycarlisle.com/ and at https://www.instagram.com/hollymcarlisle/.

Behold Through Rereading

1. Patricia Meyer Spacks, *On Rereading* (Harvard University Press, 2011).

2. Rachel Burchfield, host, *I'd Rather Be Reading*, podcast, season 14, episode 21, "Carla Jean Whitley on Her Best Books of 2024," December 29, 2024, https://tinyurl.com/3pe425k7.

3. Lydia Davis, *Essays One* (Farrar, Straus & Giroux, 2019).

Behold Through Remembering

1. Victoria Chang, *Dear Memory: Letters on Writing, Silence, and Grief* (Milkweed, 2021), 6.

2. Patricia Hampl, *The Art of the Wasted Day* (Viking, 2018), 107–8.

Behold Through Reflection

1. Diane V. Tomkinson, "Angela Foligno's Spiral Pattern of Prayer," in *Franciscans at Prayer*, ed. Timothy J. Johnson, The Medieval Franciscans 4 (Brill Academic, 2007), 198, 201–18.

2. More on Angela of Foligno's spiral pattern of prayer from Tomkinson, "Angela Foligno's Spiral Pattern of Prayer": "Angela's spiral pattern of prayer articulated a dynamic consciousness of mystical communion among herself, the Triune God and all creation in which unity and distinction coincide.

"The image of a spiral integrates the forward momentum of Angela's spiritual journey with the oscillating quality of her repeated swings between desolation and consolation. Neither the repetitive motion of a pendulum, the closed perfection of a circle, nor the ascending lines of a ladder adequately symbolize the complex interweaving of cyclical and progressive elements within Angela's mysticism. The open circles of a three-dimensional spiral better express the relational dynamism of Angela's spirituality: although she frequently described similar experiences, insights and emotions, they continually increased in both intensity and scope. Her spiraling movement in the Holy Spirit, through Christ, into the Trinity recurs and intensifies throughout the Memorial; these experiences of intensifying communion with the infinite All Good simultaneously draw the mystic into a fuller knowledge of herself and into expanding circles of relationship with the natural world, her immediate circle of spiritual companions, and the wider community of the Church both on earth and in heaven. Angela's mystical path is thus both intensively and extensively progressive. Like a powerful hurricane or tornado, the mystical spiral is in continual movement, intensifying even as it expands."

Behold Through Retreats

1. *Tiny Beautiful Things*, season 1, episode 7, "Go," written by Deirdre Shaw, aired April 7, 2023, https://tinyurl.com/23smfv56.

2. *Tiny Beautiful Things*, season 1, episode 6, "Broken Things," written by Naomi Iwamoto, aired April 7, 2023, https://tinyurl.com/44sfn2dn.

3. Several solo writing retreat guides and resources can be found at https://www.solowritingretreats.com/.

Bestow

1. *Oxford English Dictionary*, June 2025, under "bestow (verb), Etymology."

Bestow Through Both Receipt and Offering

1. Lewis Hyde, *The Gift: How Creative Spirit Transforms the World* (Vintage, 2019), 218.

2. The *Oxford English Dictionary* defines "petrifaction" as: "The action or process of hardening or immobilizing (a person or thing); a hardened or immobile condition, *esp.* a state of temporary paralysis brought on by extreme fear."

Bestow Through Words and Objects

1. The Kitchen Sisters, "Poet Emily Dickinson Was a Much Loved Baker," NPR, December 27, 2016, https://tinyurl.com/ynnnuxy6.

2. Kate Smith, "'A Trinket—to Confer': Dickinson's Poems Sent with Objects," Emily Dickinson Museum, 2023, https://tinyurl.com/2neepn8k.

Bestow Through Presence

1. Julia Cameron, *The Artist's Way* (Tarcher, 2002).

2. Markus Zusak, *The Book Thief* (Knopf, 2006).

3. Ancy Thresia N K, "Literacy and Power of Words in Markus Zusak's The Book Thief," *History Research Journal*, n.d., doi:10.26643/HRJ.V5I4.7166.

Bestow Through Story

1. Pressfield's capitalization of these terms is somewhat inconsistent. I've chosen to not capitalize "all is lost" and "epiphinal" throughout the chapter.

2. Steven Pressfield, *The Artist's Journey: The Wake of the Hero's Journey and the Lifelong Pursuit of Meaning* (Black Irish Books, 2018), 66.

3. *The Book of Common Prayer* (Church Publishing, 1979), 356–66.

4. According to Steven Pressfield, the "epiphanal moment" is "a breakthrough insight or epiphany, an awakening for the hero, an 'Aha!' moment" that almost immediately follows the "all is lost moment."

5. Steven Pressfield, *Nobody Wants to Read Your Shit* (Black Irish Books, 2016), x.

6. Jim Jarmusch, dir., *Paterson* (Amazon Studios, 2016).

7. Ethan Warren, "Watching the Wheels: Finding Meaning and Purpose in Paterson," *Bright Wall/Dark Room*, no. 32 (September 2018), https://tinyurl.com/2vuwy436.

Bestow Through Intercessory Prayer

1. Cathy Ammlung, "Intercessory Prayer, Part Two: How to Write Them," Lutheran Coalition for Renewal, January 12, 2022, https://tinyurl.com/3m2z576k.

2. "Prayer Through Writing," University of Notre Dame Campus Ministry, accessed October 6, 2025, https://tinyurl.com/4wp5ez83.

3. Rhonda Mawhood Lee, *Seek and You Will Find: Discovering a Practice of Prayer* (Forward Movement, 2021), 153.

Bestow from the Center

1. Martin Laird, *Into the Silent Land: A Guide to the Christian Practice of Contemplation* (Oxford University Press, 2006), 12.

Bestow Through Action

1. Rebecca Solnit, *Recollections of My Nonexistence: A Memoir* (Viking, 2020), 43.
2. These monthly online gatherings are hosted by https://www.portlandalano.org/.
3. Read about Attenberg's 1000 Words of Summer practice in her book *1000 Words: A Writer's Guide to Staying Creative, Focused, and Productive All Year Round* (Simon Element, 2024).

Begin Again

1. *Oxford English Dictionary*, June 2025, under "again (adv., prep., & conj.), Etymology," https://doi.org/10.1093/OED/9817s634381.
2. T. S. Eliot, *Four Quartets* (Harcourt, 1943), 50.

Begin Again with Nourishing Rhythms

1. Steven Ratiner, "Poet Mary Oliver: A Solitary Walk," *Christian Science Monitor*, December 9, 1992, https://tinyurl.com/y7p65ur6.
2. Maria Popova, "Virginia Woolf on the Creative Benefits of Keeping a Diary," *Marginalian*, January 25, 2013, https://tinyurl.com/4u6w6mue.

Charlotte Donlon is a writer, spiritual director, and gatherer whose work explores belonging in all its complexity. She holds an MFA in creative writing from Seattle Pacific University and a certificate in spiritual direction, and she invites people from diverse religious backgrounds—including skeptics—to inhabit the generative intersection of art and faith. Her essays have been published in *The Washington Post*, *The Christian Century*, *Image*, *The Millions*, and elsewhere. She lives in Birmingham, Alabama.

lon, designed by **Carol Twombly** · cover design: **HD Brewer** · book design and composition: **Lydia Christine Hall** · proofreader: **Tim Baker** · copyeditor: **Tom Raabe** · project editor: **Laurel Draper** · acquiring editor: **Lisa Ann Cockrel** · text set in **Adobe Caslo**

Here Below champions ambitious books that eschew binaries between the sacred and profane. Learn more at herebelowbooks.com.